Weird in the World

Weird in the World

Living Towards the World God Wants

J. AARON MILLER

CASCADE *Books* • Eugene, Oregon

WEIRD IN THE WORLD
Living Towards the World God Wants

Copyright © 2025 J. Aaron Miller. All rights reserved. Except for brief quotations in critical publications or reviews, no part of this book may be reproduced in any manner without prior written permission from the publisher. Write: Permissions, Wipf and Stock Publishers, 199 W. 8th Ave., Suite 3, Eugene, OR 97401.

Cascade Books
An Imprint of Wipf and Stock Publishers
199 W. 8th Ave., Suite 3
Eugene, OR 97401

www.wipfandstock.com

PAPERBACK ISBN: 979-8-3852-4267-2
HARDCOVER ISBN: 979-8-3852-4268-9
EBOOK ISBN: 979-8-3852-4269-6

Cataloguing-in-Publication data:

Names: Miller, J. Aaron, author.

Title: Weird in the world : living towards the world God wants / J. Aaron Miller.

Description: Eugene, OR : Cascade Books, 2025 | Includes bibliographical references.

Identifiers: ISBN 979-8-3852-4267-2 (paperback) | ISBN 979-8-3852-4268-9 (hardcover) | ISBN 979-8-3852-4269-6 (ebook)

Subjects: LCSH: Church. | Christianity and culture.

Classification: BV600.2 .M55 2025 (paperback) | BV600.2 (ebook)

VERSION NUMBER 11/05/25

Scripture quotations are from New Revised Standard Version Bible, copyright © 1989 National Council of the Churches of Christ in the United States of America. Used by permission. All rights reserved worldwide.

For Levi and Jude

Contents

Gratitude | ix

Introduction | xi

Signpost 1
Worship | 1

Signpost 2
Prayer | 11

Signpost 3
Incarnation | 24

Signpost 4
Discipline | 45

Signpost 5
Lament | 62

Signpost 6
Freedom | 76

The World God Wants: The Way of Jesus | 95

Epilogue | 108
Bibliography | 115

Gratitude

THE CHANCE TO WRITE even one book is a great gift. Anything more depends on the substantial love and support of many others. I am so grateful for all who have encouraged me—especially, for this project, Simon LeSieur, Dylon Nofziger, Lyn Unger, Esmeralda Cabral, Alex Wilson, Alecia Greefield, and Ross Lockhart. I am truly grateful for the congregation of University Hill United Church, with whom I get to do ministry, and who come back week after week, year after year, to wrestle with the joys and challenges of faithfulness together.

One of the great gifts of my life, and a regular source of inspiration and community, is the chance to participate in the life and work of the Vancouver School of Theology. On top of wonderful faculty and staff, every year, new students show up, in response to God's call, to give of their time, energy, and resources to pursue theological education for the sake of the church. Wonders never cease.

I'm thankful to the great folks at Cascade for taking a second chance on me, and all the work that they do in support of authors who love the church. Their gifts make ours better.

I am also eternally grateful to my parents for their determined love of the church and witness to the generous parenthood of God and the faithfulness of Christ.

Unquestionably, there are countless others who could fill my gratitude list. But it is no exaggeration to say that my life would not be nearly so blessed were it not for my wife Kate and our wonderful sons, who each reflect God's radiance to me time and again.

Introduction

IF MY CONGREGATION WERE to play "Sermon Bingo" on a Sunday morning, the "free" square in the center of the card would surely contain the phrase *"Christians are called to be weird enough in the world as it is, that when God gets the world God wants, we'll fit right in."* I say that, or something like it, most weeks. I say it over and over because I believe it's true. When St. Peter tells the church to be ready at any moment to give an account of what gives us hope, the underlying expectation is that the members of the Body of Christ are living, in some meaningful way, differently than the folks around them.[1] There ought to be something about Christians that makes our neighbors wonder what's wrong—or right—with us. We're to be the first fruits of a new possibility, an unexpected harvest.[2] We are people caught up with the God who speaks chaos into beauty, sets captives free, and raises the dead; we are called to follow the One whose life, death, resurrection, and reign signal the unstoppable coming of a new world: *the kingdom of heaven!* We are to be people with the eyes of our hearts set on that day when heaven and earth are one, and all of creation is aglow in the light of God's breathtaking love.[3]

That's the world we're to be weird for—which is easy to preach. It's even easy and occasionally inspiring to hear. The evidence suggests that it is quite a bit more challenging to live. What does it really mean to be strange in the world, when most of us need to keep our jobs,[4] and so many of us

---

1. 1 Pet 3:15.
2. Rom 8:23.
3. Rev 22:1–5.
4. I often think about this quotation from activist-theologian Brian Walsh: "A Christian can hold any job. But if they act as Christians, they will simply need to be ready to be fired within a few weeks" (Claiborne and Haw, *Jesus for President*, 241). That is maybe an easier idea to contend with as a pastor. But there are plenty of times when being too Christ-like is a risk to a stable job in paid ministry. Even the church is not always a safe place for too much Jesus.

INTRODUCTION

are overwhelmed by the demands of everyday life and the bombardments of culture, and at the end of the day most everyone I know just wants to be liked? It's nice that Jesus tells us when others utter all kinds of evil against us, then we're in the good company of the persecuted and martyred prophets before us.[5] But we'd like to avoid that if we can, honestly.

I don't think that, on the whole, the desire to avoid persecution and death is due to a lack of faith. In any church, on any given Sunday, you are likely to find people gathered who really do trust that the Way that Jesus calls us to follow, hard as it is, is the way, the truth, and the abundant life for which we are made.[6] Lots of us believe that his commitment to love (even of our enemies), forgiveness, healing, redemption, freedom, care for the least and the lost, his commitment to embodying the grace of God all the way to the grave and then through it, really is the hope of the world.

Ideally, we also create lots of space for folks who are not so sure that the Way of Jesus is the hope of the world, or who have seen too much of the world as it is to have much hope in what it will be. The Scriptures certainly invite us to wrestle with questions of faith, even when our theologies would pin us down. It's often been noted that the opposite of faith is not doubt; it's certainty. We trust in something we cannot see, much less control. We walk by faith, not by sight.[7] We're not called to know the answers—which is weird in a world enamoured of objectivity and reason and facts. Instead, we're invited into a relationship that is beautifully complex and complicated, a vulnerable and hopeful life with the Living God, whose determination is to make all things new. And we're called to live out of and for that relationship, and nothing less, in all we do.

Lots of us believe that, or something like it. Maybe we would articulate it differently, but it is awfully hard to explain the endurance of the church—even in its often-embattled state—if we don't believe that we're called, in the name and Way of Jesus, to something more and other than the world as it is. Even if some days all we can say is "I believe; help my unbelief,"[8] I don't think it's generally faith that we lack. Surely, we can scrounge up a mustard seed's worth among us.

I don't think we lack faith; I do think we often lack the imagination necessary for the things Jesus calls us to. I often lack imagination. It is much

5. Matt 5:11–12.
6. John 10:10.
7. 2 Cor 5:7.
8. Mark 9:24.

easier to conform our lives and our churches to the patterns of the world—mirroring the expectations of the surrounding social structures, organizing our communities like other corporations or not-for-profits, equating God's way with our preferred political inclinations, baptizing the expectations and predilections of our social circles—than it is to gather at the feet of the One who calls us to repentance, to transform our minds for the sake of another possibility.[9] That turning towards a new possibility, rewiring our habits and long-held assumptions, begins with a fresh imagination for how things are.

Imagination is not make-believe or naïve optimism. It is that gift and faculty that allows us to see more than what is, to live towards what is not yet, to set aside cool objectivity in favor of the wonder of the God who does more than we can conceive.[10] It's the capacity that allows us to long for something other than what is currently on offer. Karen Swallow Prior puts it like this: "We cannot desire what we cannot imagine. (We certainly can't name that desire, anyway.) If we are to envision an expression of Christian faith within our culture that is as true to Christ as can be, then we must imagine beyond the realities of our culture that limit our sight."[11]

It is always dangerous to say that the church is, or should be, one thing or another. Even our most high-minded ideals are too restrictive if we'll live in step with the Spirit who blows any-which-way.[12] But I want to insist that whatever else the church is, it ought to be a training ground for holy imagination. The church must be a place where we test out together what it looks like to express what we believe and sing and pray, in ways as "true to Christ as can be." We need all the help we can get, keeping that new heaven and earth in view. We need to learn to see what is not yet, but which is surely coming, and is the foundation of our hope for all things. We need formation in the Way that is strange in the world as it is.

Formed for What?

Formation is something I think about a lot. I am in ministry on a university campus, and often, when I get the chance, I ask academic types what an undergraduate degree is for. What's the point? I count myself among those who believe that education in general is its own reward, but most

---

9. Mark 1:15; Rom 12:2.
10. Eph 3:21. Guite, *Faith, Hope and Poetry*, 55–66.
11. Prior, *Evangelical Imagination*, 14.
12. John 3:8; Gal 5:25.

undergraduates will finish their degrees with tens of thousands of dollars in debt and not much more than the skills to undertake another degree, for which they will need more loans, so that they *might* then get a job in their field—if there are jobs to be had. It may not be as bleak as all that for everyone; anecdotally though, it's a fair assessment.

So far, everyone I have asked about the value of an undergraduate degree says something like "formation." They may not use that word, but the implication is that a student's experience in postsecondary education is meant to form them as fulsome humans in the world. Being exposed to a variety of thoughts and possibilities, being trained to think critically and expansively, gaining skills that align with one's goals, is the gateway to meaningful participation in the world. Teenagers show up with a (typically) limited worldview and restricted experience, and within three to five years they are transformed in ways that they could not have imagined when they arrived. That's the theory, anyway. And in general, I must agree that this is a good thing. The crucial season of transition from adolescence to adulthood should be a time of exploration and flourishing. It is a time of deep formation.

Except, it is not always entirely clear what students are being formed *for*. It's true that the academic context can be a bastion of revolutionary thinking, a place where people are equipped to "change the world." But, by and large, I have a hard time seeing that people are being formed by their education and their postsecondary experience for anything other than the world as it so often is: frantic, competitive, encouraging us toward acquisitiveness and overactive self-concern. Perhaps in their classes they are being liberated for something else—I certainly know some marvellous professors, whose passion, compassion, and concern for their students models another way. I have a friend who works as a counselor in the business school, whose principal concern is questions of vocation and meaning in the lives of the next generation of business leaders. I'm grateful for those witnesses. But my experience with students sitting in my office or across the table in coffee shops suggests that the practices and pace, the anxieties and expectations of campus life, as well as the industry of education, are shaping people to expect to be diabolically overworked, conformed to the patterns of late-stage capitalism, and largely committed to the principalities and powers of the current order.

So, formation matters, but not generally. It matters *what* we are being formed for. And we need to understand that we are always being formed by the world around. The types of formation that I witness on campus—and which run rampant in the world beyond, not least in the church—aren't generally the result of malicious intent of individuals or organizations. It's nearly the opposite. Formation in the ways of the world as it is stems from a *lack* of intention and a failure of imagination. We are not accidentally shaped in the Way of Jesus, but we are easily lulled into conforming to the patterns and expectations of the world around us. Walking in the Way of Jesus is a determination to be shaped not according to the way things are, but for the way that they will be. It's a practiced commitment to seeking God's kingdom first and above all.

This practice of seeking God's kingdom will look weird, whether we want it to or not. It is weird to be peacemakers in a world that is always prepared for violence. It is weird to be still and know that God is God, in a culture moving at breakneck speeds in the service of myriad idols. It is weird to be people of faithfulness when we are immersed in algorithms designed to distract us with the next fleeting thing. It is weird to be people of hope when everything seems to be going up in flames. It is weird to be a people of self-giving love, when we have been so well-trained to be people of self-indulgence and self-concern. It is weird to find our truest identity in Christ, not our accomplishments and accolades and personal expression.

It's telling that, throughout the Gospels, the disciples continually revert to old, familiar patterns of behavior—even though they spend every waking moment in the company of Jesus. They are overcome by fear and geared up for violence, overwhelmed by "the lure of wealth and the cares of the world,"[13] unable to imagine that the Way of the Cross can possibly counteract the Ways of Empire.[14] Of course, we have the advantage of following Jesus on the other side of the resurrection. But John's Gospel shows us that even after meeting the risen Jesus and receiving the Holy Spirit, the disciples are quick to go back to what they know. Commissioned and literally inspired by the resurrected Lord, they decided to go fishing.[15] They pick up where they left off before this Jesus adventure began.

It isn't any easier or more straightforward for us to hear Jesus's call and live it than it was for them. We are still quick to call down fire on those who disagree with or disparage us. We reach for weapons when violence threatens. We hear Jesus's call to pick up our crosses but determine that there must be a less demanding and painful way, a more pleasant and efficient

---

13. Matt 13:22.
14. Luke 9:54; Mark 4:19; Matt 16:21–23.
15. John 21:3.

way to shape our lives. We marvel at the beauty of the temples we make and fail to take seriously our lives and bodies as temples of the Holy Spirit. The fickleness, the double-mindedness, the lukewarm life of the earliest churches are perfectly recognizable in our own time and place. Every one of us still sins and falls short of the glory of God.[16]

So, we must begin with grace. One of the most essential things the church does is come together to acknowledge our sin—all the ways we fail to love God and neighbor with everything we've got—and then we proclaim the tireless grace of God, to heal and restore and send us out again. We approach the throne of mercy boldly, not because we are bold, but because of the relentless love of the One who beckons us.[17] And still, we are every bit as likely to cheapen that grace as Christians have ever been.[18] We are as ever in search of the loophole of grace as the first churches were,[19] which means that we miss out on the fullness of God's grace for us, the wild height and depth, the astonishing length and width of God's love for us.[20] We treat God's grace as a "get out of jail free" card when we mess up, when it is actually the perfect freedom to get after what God is after in all we do—in victory and failure. If all we want is a loophole, we'll never find that narrow gate that leads to life abundant. Though we depend on grace, we are also called to conform our lives to its pattern.

Certainly, in the Christian life "the indicative 'you are' always comes before the imperative 'you ought'": Jesus tells us who we are before telling us what we ought to do.[21] But it's an impoverished life if there is no "ought." If we believe the things we sing and pray, read and hear, teach and preach on a Sunday morning, then there are serious implications for more than that hour or two that we spend in worship. We're made for more than a yo-yo diet of cheap grace and empty spiritual calories. We're made to get the gospel into our bones and muscles, to grow up into the fullness of Christ, to incarnate the hope that is ours, to let our lives shine as beacons of another way.

The challenge, though, is realigning our vision of what is truly worth doing. We are well, if passively, trained by the culture around us in certain ways of doing and achieving, of attributing value and measuring returns

16. Rom 3:23.
17. Heb 4:16.
18. Bonhoeffer, *Discipleship*, 3.
19. Rom 6:1, etc.
20. Eph 3:14–21.
21. Willimon, *Remember Who You Are*, 29.

INTRODUCTION

on investment. But a church growing in the Way of Jesus is not going to reflect the instilled values and expectations of a culture that is often set up in opposition to the peculiar call of the One refuses to grasp at the familiar markers of success and power. A church growing in the Way of Jesus will look as strange as the God who empties himself for love's sake.[22] We need a regularly refreshed imagination for what the alternative Way of Jesus looks like. We need signposts on the way to gospel strangeness.

A Song for the Strange

I confess that I often skim over or ignore the superscripts of the psalms, the little details that introduce many of the prayers in the psalter, which often tell us about the author, or how the prayer is meant to be accompanied. But at some point, I was struck by something I had ignored countless times: the superscript that introduces Ps 34. It reads: *Of David, when he feigned madness before Abimelech, so that he drove him out, and he went away.* It's a peculiar setup for the prayer that follows it, which has no obvious connection to the story it references from 1 Sam 21. In that story, David is on the run from Saul and lands in the Philistine territory of King Achish of Gath. The king's advisors point out that David is the same guy who has made a career of killing Philistines so successfully that the Israelites made musicals, complete with choreography, to celebrate him. Needless to say, David gets worried that this might not be the safest place to hide out. He decides that the best response is to pretend to be a madman, someone who poses no threat to the Philistine order. He plays the part exceptionally, right down to drooling over his beard and clawing at doors. It's an Oscar-worthy performance. King Achish sees this and tells his servants that they have enough of their own madmen to take care of around these parts and to chase this one off. Which is what happens. So, David escapes.

Again, it's hard to see what this story has to do with the prayer that we know as Ps 34. But, given my conviction that Christians are supposed to be strange enough in this world that, when God gets the world God wants, we'll fit right in, I began to wonder if perhaps what connects the prayer and the story is David's apparent madness. I began to wonder if this is a prayer that shapes us in the strange ways of God—ways that look like lunacy to the kings and powers of the world as we know it. It's obviously a bit of an interpretive stretch, and the goal of Christian life is not to *pretend* to be weird

22. Phil 2:5–11.

INTRODUCTION

like Jesus; we *are to be* weird like Jesus. Even so, the more that I have let the idea percolate, the more it feels like this really is a Song for the Strange, a resource for developing an imagination for the way we live and move and have our being in the world, in the Way of Jesus. I think Ps 34 is a prayer that shapes us to be weird in the world. While David's acting for Achish (or Abimelech . . . ?)[23] strikes me as a spontaneous, anxiety induced, by-the-seat-of-his-pants strategy, his prayer is deeply deliberate. It invites us into rhythms of holiness that are at odds with so much of what surrounds us. In the end, I can't help but wonder if David's physical spontaneity, bizarre as it was successful, was the result of his disciplined spiritual commitment to pursuing the God who had pursued him. The prayer reveals the background against which David moved strangely in the world. It doesn't narrate or retell the story it references; it makes sense of it.[24]

Importantly, this psalm is an acrostic poem, based on the letters of the Hebrew alphabet. That kind of mnemonic device suggests strongly that this is a prayer that is meant to be easily memorized. It is catechetical: it's the ABCs of a God-soaked faith. Psalm 34 guides us through a liturgy for life that is strange in this world and eager for the one to come; it offers us "signposts" on the way to gospel strangeness. Reading it through a Christian lens, the psalmist calls us to look to that day when all people will gather on the banks of the River of Life, flowing from heaven's throne, when we will rejoice at the foot of the Tree of Life, bearing fruit in every season and whose leaves are for the healing of the nations. And this prayer leads us in a living response to that vision, that promise, now.[25] It grounds us in the ways of worship and prayer, incarnation and discipline, lament and ultimate freedom—not just freedom *from* what holds us captive, but *for* the reign of God and nothing less. The chapters that follow are meant to be part of a conversation with this ancient prayer, for the cultivation of a Christian imagination of what it means to live in the world in step with God. This is not a technical commentary but an attempt to listen and respond to what the Holy Spirit has to say to us, wherever we find ourselves, through David's ancient words.

---

23. Some scholars argue that these names are interchangeable, belonging to the same king. I like to entertain the idea that the Holy Spirit is content to work through our missteps and typos.

24. Rowe, *Leading Christian Communities*, 36.

25. Rev 22.

INTRODUCTION

There is much more to say about each of the topics below than I have space or wisdom to offer. Given that, I want to think about each signpost that I see in Ps 34 through four lenses. The signposts are: Worship, Prayer, Incarnation, Discipline, Lament, and Freedom, and each is weird, political, an act of presence, and a way of life. These are not by any stretch the only ways to think about these things, nor are they exclusive from one another—each one overlaps with the others. Undoubtedly, each can lead to another way of thinking, envisioning, and exploring the narrow way that leads to God's wide-open grace. I hope to offer what follows as an invitation to enter a little deeper into the living conversation, to cultivate an imagination about what it means to walk in the weird and wonderful Way of Jesus.

> Psalm 34 NRSV
> Of David, when he feigned madness before Abimelech, so that he drove him out, and he went away.
> 1 I will bless the Lord at all times;
> his praise shall continually be in my mouth.
> 2 My soul makes its boast in the Lord;
> let the humble hear and be glad.
> 3 O magnify the Lord with me,
> and let us exalt his name together.
> 4 I sought the Lord, and he answered me
> and delivered me from all my fears.
> 5 Look to him, and be radiant,
> so your faces shall never be ashamed.
> 6 This poor soul cried and was heard by the Lord
> and was saved from every trouble.
> 7 The angel of the Lord encamps
> around those who fear him and delivers them.
> 8 O taste and see that the Lord is good;
> happy are those who take refuge in him.
> 9 O fear the Lord, you his holy ones,
> for those who fear him have no want.
> 10 The young lions suffer want and hunger,
> but those who seek the Lord lack no good thing.
> 11 Come, O children, listen to me;
> I will teach you the fear of the Lord.
> 12 Which of you desires life
> and covets many days to enjoy good?
> 13 Keep your tongue from evil
> and your lips from speaking deceit.

14 Depart from evil, and do good;
seek peace, and pursue it.
15 The eyes of the Lord are on the righteous,
and his ears are open to their cry.
16 The face of the Lord is against evildoers,
to cut off the remembrance of them from the earth.
17 When the righteous cry for help, the Lord hears
and rescues them from all their troubles.
18 The Lord is near to the brokenhearted
and saves the crushed in spirit.
19 Many are the afflictions of the righteous,
but the Lord rescues them from them all.
20 He keeps all their bones;
not one of them will be broken.
21 Evil brings death to the wicked,
and those who hate the righteous will be condemned.
22 The Lord redeems the life of his servants;
none of those who take refuge in him will be condemned.

Signpost 1

Worship

And whenever the living creatures give glory and honor and thanks to the one who is seated on the throne, who lives forever and ever, the twenty-four elders fall before the one who is seated on the throne and worship the one who lives forever and ever; they cast their crowns before the throne, singing, "You are worthy, our Lord and God, to receive glory and honor and power, for you created all things, and by your will they existed and were created."

REVELATION 4:9–11

I will bless the LORD at all times; his praise shall continually be in my mouth. My soul makes its boast in the LORD; let the humble hear and be glad. O magnify the LORD with me, and let us exalt his name together.

PSALM 34:1–3

Worship Is Weird

WORSHIP IS WEIRD NOT just because we get together regularly to offer time and money for purposes that may or may not be of obvious personal benefit, which is absurd compared to the values acquisition and self-concern that permeate so many of the spaces that we occupy. Worship is weird, not just because of the peculiar elements of our given traditions, which can range from bizarre to incomprehensible, even for many who practice them.

But worship is weird mostly for the fact of worshiping at all, in a world that regularly feels like it's coming apart at the seams. Listening to the news of another government bombing their neighbors, or the increasing political strife that threatens so many countries, or environmental catastrophes, or whatever local threat is making headlines this week, you could forgive someone for wondering how we Christians can show up and give praise to the God who often seems absent at best, or indifferent at worst. How do we sing "Praise to the Lord, the Almighty," when everything is on fire and relief seems so elusive?[1]

It's a reasonable question, and every generation of disciples has had its own version of it to wrestle with. If our worship becomes little more than spiritual anesthetic for the hurts of the world and wounds in our souls, then we're missing the point. What's more, worship that has no place for lament, for heartbreak, and for things to just not be okay is out of step with the long witness of the church and her weeping Lord.[2] We'll see, later in the psalm, that to be weird in the Way of Jesus has nothing to do with spiritual escapism or avoiding the pains of the world.

However, if our worship is predicated on the right circumstances, if we are only able to worship when everything is okay, then we're starting from the wrong end of things. The fact that Ps 34 begins by leading us in worship, calling us together to join our voices with the numberless throng of saints and angels around heaven's throne,[3] tells us something important about what worship really is. It's not just about appeasing God, or getting God to look favorably on us, or even giving thanks to God for all we are and have. Worship is mostly a matter of orientation: it's turning towards the One who has turned towards us in love. It's learning to begin from that love, over anything else, and to be formed by it. What's particularly weird about worship is that it is not contingent on what's going on in or around us. We don't have to be in the right mood. The world doesn't have to be in order. Our lives don't have to be going the way that we wish they would, because worship is not about us. It shapes us, but it's not about us.

Worship is not about us and it's not really *about* God, either. That may seem an unlikely thing to say, but our language here is important. If we imagine worship to be "about God," it can quickly devolve into theological information disguised as praise. That can be pleasing to us, as people

---

1. Neander, "Praise to the Lord, the Almighty."
2. John 11:35.
3. Rev 7:9.

who have been led to believe that knowledge is power and with the right, objective answers we can solve all the problems of the world. But God is not the answer to our problems; God is God. And worship is, first of all, an encounter with the Living God. Worship is the way in which we learn to start with God as God, the ultimate Thou to our I, the truly Other who is worthy of our praise.[4]

Worship is the act of coming into the presence of the God who, in Jesus and by the Holy Spirit, has promised to be with us always, "even to the end of the age."[5] It's drawing near to the God who makes promises and keeps them. It's leaning into the promise that all we are is not all there is—not by a long shot. It's refusing to start with the mess of things, or the way we wish they were, and starting instead by turning our eyes to the One whose Spirit is not overwhelmed by chaos, but whose first act in Scripture is to turn chaos into beauty. We start with the One who will not force a new world by power and violence but draws forth the wholeness of things by divine invitation: "Let there be," not "Make it so!"[6]

And it's learning always to begin there, so that we can live from there. David's determination to keep God's praise continually in his mouth is a poetic way of describing the primacy of his relationship to God, who is worthy of praise, worthy of honor and power and glory, whose ways and thoughts are far above ours. It's his life lived in antiphonal response to the songs that echo around heaven's throne. David is obviously not constantly singing worship songs every second of the day; he's not reciting liturgies to himself or speaking as if he were eternally in worship leader mode. That would be weird, for sure, but not faithful, because that's not what continual worship looks like. Instead, David is, however and always humanly, learning to do whatever he does, in word or deed, towards the glory of God. He is being formed for the world as it will be, when God gets what God wants.

Worship Is Political

As we think about what it means to be weird in the world as it is, it matters that David is on his way to being Israel's king and that this is a psalm sung in remembrance of his tense interaction with a rival king. It matters because it points us to the fact that worship is an essentially political act. Worship is a

4. Buber, *I and Thou*.
5. Matt 28:20.
6. Crouch, *Playing God*, 31.

practice that forms a *polis*, shapes a people for a particular way of being in the world that is different from, and often at odds with, the politics of the world around. Worship may or may not make us better citizens of the nation we find ourselves in. We might be grateful for the country in which we live, but national pride is too narrow a category for the kingdom of God. Whatever national anthems might claim about God's provision and care for the state and its people, the biblical vision is unconstrained by borders and constitutions. God does not seem to be interested in stopping at making one particular nation great; but God is after a people who will be the "living stones" with which the kingdom of God will be built, on earth as in heaven, until that day when heaven and earth are one.[7] St. Peter gives us a vision of the whole church—not any one congregation, but all those who have been called and claimed by Christ—as a new multinational, multiethnic, multilinguistic political reality coming together in the rubble of the old order of things:

> But you are a chosen race, a royal priesthood, a holy nation, God's own people, in order that you may proclaim the mighty acts of him who called you out of darkness into his marvelous light. Once you were not a people, but now you are God's people; once you had not received mercy, but now you have received mercy.[8]

Being formed as the people of God is at the heart of things whenever we show up in worship. That's how we should imagine our congregations, whoever is with us and however many are there. Whether two or three are gathered in quiet prayer, or ten thousand are raising their voices together, truly worshiping together is to pledge allegiance to nothing less than the kingdom of God and to open ourselves to being shaped accordingly. As James K. A. Smith puts it:

> Christian worship is [an] inherently a *political* act. The proclamation of the Word is the rehearsal of a liberation narrative for a royal priesthood, the announcement of a *euangelion* that rivals Caesar's. The Table is a revolutionary meal in which even the "are nots" are invited to sit at the King's table. The weekly gathering of the saints is a rite that rehearses their heavenly citizenship.[9]

Citizenship is one of the more important and revolutionary themes in the New Testament. Citizenship certainly matters today, but for the people

---

7. 1 Pet 2:4–5.
8. 1 Pet 2:9–10.
9. Smith, *Awaiting the King*, 58.

to whom Paul and Peter and the others were writing, it was an especially serious thing. In the Roman Empire, to be a Roman citizen meant access to the rights and privileges of the empire. It meant certain protections and freedoms. Roman citizenship was coveted. It defined a person as in or out, in important, life or death ways. Citizenship came with the responsibility to live and act in ways appropriate to, and honoring of, the privilege of being Roman. A Roman citizen was expected, in their limited way, to represent the goals, ethics, and glory of the empire.

So, when we hear the early church claiming a new citizenship,[10] that's not just an initiation into a new club. Belonging to the church is not just an opportunity to get personalized offering envelopes or vote at their church's AGM. It's not about the perks of membership. It's an act of defiance, an articulation of the promise that in Christ we are not subject to the whims and demands and expectations of the emperor or his underlings—or restricted by any other political arrangement. We are seeking God's will on earth as it is in heaven. Our citizenship is rooted in the promise that "God is out to make for himself a people who reflect his holiness, who are marked by righteousness, and who live in justice and the shalom of God."[11] In Christ, we are perfectly free to pursue the goals and glory of God, come what may.

And *come what may* is important, because what may come is a cross, the ultimate punishment for stepping out of line with the empire—Jesus seemed to be pretty insistent about this, in fact.[12] But, as St. Paul puts it, "[God] disarmed the rulers and authorities and made a public example of them, triumphing over them in [the cross]."[13] The church does not gather in fearful submission to the principalities and powers of this or any age; we gather in the promise that the worst they can throw at us is a childish temper tantrum compared to the glory of God. We don't gather in fear of the cross, but in the hope of resurrection and the unstoppable coming of the kingdom of God.

With fondness, I remember being at the Greenbelt Festival, in Cheltenham, England, in 2013.[14] This festival is a sort of funhouse for church nerds and spiritual seekers. It is a multi-day experience, with opportunities to hear from leading thinkers in the church, explore a dizzying array of faith

---

10. Phil 3:20, for instance.
11. Smith, *Called to Be Saints*, 18.
12. Matt 10:38, 16:42; Mark 8:34; Luke 9:23, 14:27.
13. Col 2:15.
14. https://www.greenbelt.org.uk/.

practices, along with music from a wide range of artists and choirs ranging from evangelical Christian to vaguely spiritual.[15] One of the highlights of the time is an event called "Beer and Hymns," which is exactly what it sounds like. In the middle of the week, we crammed into a huge tent with 1,500 of our new closest friends, with plastic cups of beer procured from the makeshift Jesus Arms Pub, and we sang some of history's best hymns together. At one point, they decided that we should sing a Christmas carol, even though it was the middle of August. But together we launched into "Hark the Herald Angels Sing." When we got to the final verse there were enough sopranos in the crowd who knew the descant by heart, which soared over the rest of us. It was a surreal experience, standing in the middle of the Cheltenham Racetrack, in a country known for its increasing secularity, singing praises at the top of our lungs. It was a deeply political moment. We were uninhibited in our worship, not so much because of the beer, but simply by the opportunity, even for a short time, to raise our voices in "wonder, love, and praise" with a sea of others who wanted to do the same.[16] For a little while we caught a sense of what it will be like around heaven's throne, caught up in the glory of the God who made, sustains, loves, and saves every piece of creation.

Worship Is Presence, Not Entertainment

It has to be said that if one were to wander into an average church on any given Sunday, one might be forgiven for not realizing that the congregation was, at any point in the service, caught up in "wonder, love, and praise" of the God who is supremely worthy of our wholehearted devotion, or that this gathering is an exuberant declaration of a new cosmic order. The comedian Eddie Izzard (also known as Suzy Izzard[17]), an avowed atheist, has a bit about hymn singers in the Church of England who manage to sing hallelujahs while sounding utterly bored.[18] It's depressingly funny. Although an atheist comedian may seem like an ignorable commentator on the state of worship in the church, he's got some serious ecclesiastical

---

15. The year that I was there, Graham Kendrick was one of the well-known evangelicals to take part. I had no idea that singing "Shine Jesus, Shine" with Graham Kendrick was on my bucket list, but my United Church summer-camp-kid heart was thrilled.

16. Wesley, *Voices United*, 333.

17. Del Rosario, "Call Her Suzy." Izzard identifies as gender fluid and continues to alternate between "Eddie" and "Suzy."

18. To watch this particular bit: Izzard, "Christian Singing."

allies on this point. No less a figure than John Wesley encourages us to sing hymns "lustily and with good courage," but how often can we truly apply those adjectives to our singing?[19] Wesley and Izzard are an odd couple by any measure, but together they tell us something about what is, or should be, going on in worship. It doesn't seem to matter what tradition or style (though perhaps some are more conducive to courageous lustiness than others), there's always a chance and danger that people will worship with the same enthusiasm that we might bring to filing our taxes—as if it's the sort of thing we feel like we should do, but nobody really wants to, and it kind of puts a kink in the weekend.

It's oddly hopeful that there has never been a follower of Jesus who has not found themselves worshiping with less than everything they've got at some point or another. And perhaps we can be forgiven for not always being completely present where our bodies are, or adequately attentive to the circumstances we find ourselves in, in the presence of God. Moreover, worship should certainly be a space where the weary and burdened find themselves in the embrace of the One who grants us rest, which should keep us from trying to manufacture energy and enthusiasm. There is no biblical precedent for whipping ourselves into a worshipful frenzy. Within the scriptural story, only the priests of Baal resort to that sort of thing.[20] But if I venture a guess as to why our worship is not always reflective of the wonder and glory of the One to whom we are offering our praise, my suspicion is that the church, like so much in our lives, is overwhelmed by the cultural expectation of passive entertainment. We can barely help but expect that a worship service will entertain us, move us, inspire worshipful feelings, without demanding anything of us.

This might be more of a problem in mainline traditions like mine where we have so prized the professionalism of clergy, a structure that invites the outsourcing of our baptismal vows, as a friend of mine puts it.[21] We tend to be more reserved, more reasonable and rational, following the lead of clergy with university degrees, who have been trained in handling holy things for us. But I have also spent enough time in hand-raising evangelical churches to have found myself in that awkward, voyeuristic time, when the worship leader seems to be having a private worship moment,

---

19. Wesley, *Voices United*, 720.
20. Peterson, *Jesus Way*, 110. See 1 Kgs 18:28.
21. This is Rev. Dr. Ross Lockhart's line. Ross is dean of St. Andrew's Hall and professor of missional leadership at the Vancouver School of Theology.

while the rest of us stand there trying to figure out what to do until the next verse starts. Worship of any type can be turned into religious performance.

In any case, if the music isn't the style that we like, or the prayers don't inspire feelings of devotion, or the sermon falls flat or doesn't address the things we think it should (or the preacher spends too much time addressing things we think they shouldn't), or we stayed up too late last night and the kids were annoying this morning, then it's just easier to plan our shopping lists, or make notes of all the ways we disagree with what's being said or done, or simply count the minutes until we can get on to the next thing. And I do think that worship leaders, liturgists, presiders, and preachers have a responsibility for doing their work in ways that evidence the seriousness of what we're up to when we gather. We ought to prepare expecting the Holy Spirit to use our efforts to grow up our communities in Christ. We have every reason to bring our best to worship leadership.

But, it's not actually the responsibility of the people at the front to make a congregation worship. Sure, we want to facilitate, to create space. We have a particular, covenanted responsibility to point in word and deed to the One who is worthy of our praise. But worship—and worship leadership—is primarily an act of discipleship. It's seeking after the One who has sought us, drawing near to God, trusting that when we do so, God will draw near to us.[22] And nobody can do that for us. Nobody can be encountered by, or encounter, Jesus for us, thanks be to God. We each have a responsibility for how we arrive and for what we're prepared to let the Spirit do in us. It is easy to pick apart any service, any sermon, any musical selection, looking for ways that it could have been better or at least more interesting. It is much harder to trust the Spirit of God to speak through the feeble words of a fellow disciple. It is much harder to allow that the liturgies that have shaped followers of Jesus for centuries, in times and places much different from ours, might also shape us in our time and place. It's much harder to let the Spirit give us an imagination for the fact that this little group of people, being led by a slightly out of tune piano, or even the stadium singing along with pop-star worship leaders, is adding its own joyful noise to the choirs of heaven.

What difference would it make if we entered each worship gathering under the cover of the prayer: *God, let me hear what you have for me this morning*? What if we trusted that the Spirit of the Living God really is prepared to be alive to us in the Scriptures and the Sacraments, made known

22. Jas 4:8.

to us in hymns and prayers and even lackluster preaching? Let's remember that St. Paul's preaching was so long and boring that he nearly killed a guy, and St. Peter's Pentecost sermon was nothing to write home about.[23] But who can imagine the church without Paul? And Peter baptized three thousand people that day. Somehow the kingdom of heaven broke loose through their ministries anyway, almost in spite of themselves. When we show up to worship, the goal isn't spiritual entertainment, but an encounter with the God who is, even now, gathering all things to himself, setting captives free and raising the dead, making all things new. It's to come together believing that when we gather in the name of Jesus, even just two of us, Jesus himself will be there just like he promised. And when that happens, who knows what else might?

Worship Is a Way of Life

We generally think about worship as the regular gathering of people, together for an hour or two, to turn our attention corporately to God. There is no substitute for this spiritual practice. We are not meant to follow Jesus alone. We are not meant for a merely private spirituality. The writer of Hebrews warns us against the spiritual danger of ceasing to meet in community.[24] As David leads us in Ps 34, his ultimate invitation is to "magnify the LORD with me, and let us exalt his name *together*."[25] We need the encouragement that comes from knowing that we're not the only ones trying to get after the weird Way of Jesus. However, we need to attend to the flow into and out of corporate worship. David is not witnessing to the value of an hour or two a week. He's teaching us that corporate worship is both the result of and catalyst for a life of worship.

David is learning to bless the LORD at all times, keeping God's praise continually in his mouth. Which is to say that he's working to let his whole life be shaped by encounter with the Living God. Too often we expect Sunday morning to do the heavy lifting of Christian formation, as if an hour a week can contend with the content of the other 167 on its own. Frankly, part of the reason we may find ourselves nonplussed by the average worship service is that every week it feels like we're starting again something that should be a continual process and practice. It often seems like we have to

---

23. Acts 20:9–12; 2:14–36.
24. Heb 10:25.
25. Italics added.

gear up to do something entirely different than what we've been doing since the last time we were here, and sometimes we just don't have the energy or the desire to move from the supposedly secular to the apparently sacred. But worship isn't meant to be an isolated experience, once a week, or a few times a month, or (increasingly) a couple of times a year; it's not a break from whatever else we get up to. It's meant to be part of the natural rhythm of response to the call of God in all that we do.

Worship forms a kind of hub around which the rest of our life naturally turns. Our communal worship is animated by our regular and intentional spiritual practices outside of Sunday morning: times of personal prayer, Scripture reading, and worship in the quiet moments of our lives, and our faithful and fumbling apprenticeship to Jesus within the business of our days. From there, it is a wonderful thing to come into the presence of others who have been seeking God's face on their own, attending to God's presence through the ups and downs of everyday life, and now simply want to enjoy magnifying God's name together—or return, in the company of others, to the One who will be a shelter in the midst of life's storms and battles. And from our worship we move back into the world to begin to practice the things we've said and sung and prayed together.

Christian worship provides the imaginative framework for what abundant life in the Way of Jesus looks like, on the ground, in our homes, at our workplaces, as we make our way in the world. Any worship that doesn't find its way into offices or playgrounds, classrooms or checkout lines is incomplete, because worship and formation go hand in hand. What we do together must find expression when we're apart. Even better: What we do together is *meant* to find expression when we're apart. We *get* to incorporate the wonder of God into our work and our play; we get to cling to the grace and mercy that is proclaimed over us in all our victories and failures; we get to allow the Scriptures to shape our lives, setting our stories within the story of God; we get to sing our songs of praise and lament and hope so that they echo through all our interactions; we get to bind up our words in the prayers we've prayed, so that God's praise is continually in our mouths; we get to taste the wine and bread that sustains us in the Way of Jesus, carrying the death of Christ in our bodies so that the life of Christ might be visible in us.[26] We don't always do these things. But we are free to.

---

26. 2 Cor 4:10.

Signpost 2

Prayer

We today yearn for prayer and hide from prayer. We are attracted to it and repelled by it. We believe prayer is something we should do, even something we want to do, but it seems like a chasm stands between us and actually praying. We experience the agony of prayerlessness.[1]

I sought the LORD and he answered me, and delivered me from all my fears.
Look to him, and be radiant; so your faces shall never be ashamed.

PSALM 34:5

Prayer Is Weird

THERE'S NOT REALLY ANY way around it: prayer is weird. I have had more than one skeptic tell me that prayer is some kind of delusion—talking to an imaginary friend or taking my interior monologues a little too seriously, that what I feel is just emotional projection, and when my prayers and my circumstances align that's nothing more than happy coincidence. Even for many believers, prayer is a thorny issue in a "disenchanted age" like ours.[2] Perhaps we are encouraged, even inspired, by St. Paul's insistence that we have every reason to let go of all anxiety and instead, "in everything by

---

1. Foster, *Prayer*, 7.
2. Taylor, *Secular Age*.

prayer and petition, with thanksgiving, present your requests to God."[3] But for many of us prayer is a last resort, not a first response. We have strategic plans and credit cards and our own best efforts to get through before we get to prayer.

And yet, the idea of trying to follow Jesus, embodying his strange way in the world, is biblically inconceivable without prayer. It should be obvious that we cannot learn to do what he does, we cannot apprentice under him, without *doing what he does*.[4] How often is Jesus found off in some quiet place, early in the morning, praying? At the highpoints and most fearsome moments of his ministry his default is prayer. In rejoicing, he prays. When he's exhausted from the demands of the crowds, he retreats into prayer. In agony and fear, he prays. The only thing his disciples ever explicitly ask him to teach them is how to pray.[5] I would have been inclined to ask how to do miracles, or maybe preach in such a way that crowds follow me around. But the disciples seem to recognize that all the stuff Jesus does, which captures the attention and imagination of people everywhere he goes, flows out of a deep well of prayer.[6] And so, "Lord, teach us to pray."

Still, surely it was easier for those first disciples, shaped by a worldview that not only allowed for God's intervention in time and space, but assumed it. We moderns find ourselves restricted by what the philosopher Charles Taylor calls "the immanent frame."[7] Very simply, we are trapped in a vision of things that only truly allows for what is visible, testable, predictable, physical. We may have some "spiritual" inclinations, but those belong in private, no more than idiosyncratic quirks. Because of our historical location, in most places in the increasingly secular West, outside of a sanctuary or small group meeting, it's usually very weird when someone openly admits that they have been praying about anything. A friend of mine suggests that if you want a seat on the bus just tell the folks around you that you talk to God, and God talks to you. That will almost certainly clear some space.

Prayer is weird, but I think Richard Foster is on to something when he says that we both yearn for prayer and hide from it. We may spend our days in the immanent frame, but we are also, Taylor says, "haunted by

---

3. Phil 4:6.
4. Comer, *Practicing the Way*, 124.
5. Luke 11:1.
6. Comer, "Prayer Practice."
7. Taylor, *Secular Age*, 539.

transcendence."[8] We long for something, or Someone, beyond ourselves. To that end, saints in every generation have insisted that prayer is the central act of a life lived towards God—which is not to say that there is not a peculiar wisdom in our wariness about it. To pray is to enter a reality that we cannot control. It is a sacrifice of our autonomy. As David leads us in prayer, we are confronted both with the glory of God's salvation and the reality that we are desperately in need of a power not our own. "I sought the Lord and he answered me" is an extraordinary fact. *And* it lays bare the fact that we need something we cannot work up ourselves. To pray is to come into the presence of the One whose ways and thoughts are high above ours, which is a wondrous and risky proposition.[9]

But perhaps we're ready for that risk. While the immanent frame is a looming reality for most of us, anecdotally, it seems to me that it's developing cracks. In my experience with both university students and mainline congregation members, there is a tentative but increasing desire to experience that "more" that we see played out on the pages of Scripture and in the lives of the heroes of the church. A purely rational faith is not only impossible—we cannot whittle the God of all things down to a manageable size—but also, it's not especially desirable for most people. We may be trained to be wary of stuff that is too weird, we may temper our hopes when it comes to miracles, we may (rightly, I believe) seek out medical expertise before assuming that every sickness is a demon to be prayed away. Still, the scriptural invitation to a life of prayer captures the heart and releases the imagination for a world that looks radically different than we have been led to believe is possible. The book of Acts seems way more fun than most of our church experiences. The stuff Paul assumes will be a part of the life of any congregation growing in Christlikeness—gifts of the Spirit, world altering prayers, life lived in vigorous step with God—sounds both unnerving and exhilarating. We might be skeptical of bread blessed and multiplied, or water turned to wine, but is there nothing in us that yearns for more than we can ask or imagine?[10]

There's a story about John Wimber, founder of the Vineyard Church, who was dramatically converted to Christ from a life of youthful dissolution. Newly in love with Jesus, he attended some mainline Protestant churches. But when he asked, "When do you do the healings, the exorcisms, and

---

8. Smith, *How (Not) to Be Secular*, 1.
9. Isa 55:8–9.
10. Mark 6:30–44; John 2:1–11; Eph 3:21.

stuff?"—the things he had read about in the Bible—he was told, "Oh, we believe in those things, but we don't do them." John replied in amazement, "I gave up drugs for this?!"[11] Of course, the wilder workings of the Spirit are definitely not the only way to mark the presence of God, and I trust that there are many who are nurtured in faith by the comfort and familiarity of liturgy, by the simple and priceless gift of steady spiritual community. But I wonder if we reasonable mainliners are not hindered in our growth, both in breadth and depth, by a (too often explicit) desire to keep God at a safe distance. We keep ourselves from being "filled with all the fullness of God" by setting respectable limits on just how filled we can be.[12] But, why would the world want anything to do with the church if we have nothing more to offer than a tamed and nostalgic spirituality, something to believe but not do, an experience far less intriguing than any number of narcotic options available? And why should we settle for that?

The movement from comfort and tameness to being filled with all the fullness of God begins in prayer. It begins by drawing near to the One who has drawn wondrously near to us, stewarding our time so that we can connect with intention and loving leisureliness to the God who made us and knows us better than we know ourselves, and who, by grace, will lead us into the lives for which we long.

Prayer Is Political

Like worship, prayer is political—literally forming a *polis*, a people, for a new world order. Prayer is the primary practice by which the church discovers and recovers its identity as a Spirit-filled community, a Body revealing the ways and means of God in the world.[13] The grounding petition in the central prayer of the Sermon on the Mount is "Your kingdom come, your will be done, on earth as in heaven." The reality that sparks Christian imagination, that compels and propels a life shaped in the Way of Jesus, is the promise that there is coming a day when the realm of God will be as clear in our neighborhoods as around the throne of heaven. And more

---

11. Niclosi, *Culture Shift*, 27.

12. Eph 3:19.

13. LeSieur, "Come, Holy Spirit," 53. LeSieur's doctor of ministry thesis is an important exploration of "what happens when a small group of people begin to reincorporate an expectant and intentional awareness of the Holy Spirit into their life and work" (53).

immediately, we are agents and ambassadors of that future here and now. In us, that future is already present.

As Jesus teaches us to pray for God's kingdom, he creates in us the conditions for joyful obedience and loving surrender to the ways and means of God. To pray for all of heaven on earth is to pray for the world we most desperately want. It's to put our trust, our hope, our lives in the hands of the One whose deep desire is for our healing, wholeness, and flourishing. We do not pray to or for a distant ruler whose goal is to tinker with things at arm's length. We open ourselves up to the God whose end goal is unity with us. When St. John catches a glimpse of what we are waiting for, the day we are invited to live for, he describes it like this:

> Then I saw a new heaven and a new earth; for the first heaven and the first earth had passed away, and the sea was no more. And I saw the holy city, the new Jerusalem, coming down out of heaven from God, prepared as a bride adorned for her husband. And I heard a loud voice from the throne saying: "See, the home of God is among mortals. He will dwell with them; they will be his peoples, and God himself will be with them; he will wipe away every tear from their eyes. Death will be no more; mourning and crying and pain will be no more, for the first things have passed away...."
>
> I saw no temple in the city, for its temple is the Lord God the Almighty and the Lamb. And the city has no need of sun or moon to shine on it, for the glory of God is its light, and its lamp is the Lamb. The nations will walk by its light, and the kings of the earth will bring their glory into it. Its gates will never be shut by day, and there will be no night there. People will bring into it the glory and the honour of the nations. But nothing unclean will enter it.[14]

If that's the future that is pulling us towards itself, then how we order our lives together in the present ought to reflect it. A people learning to be filled with all the fullness of God will image the city overwhelmed by the glory and goodness of God. We will be people eager for renewal, both of ourselves and our communities, committed to mutual flourishing. We will seek to be among those who come alongside the broken-hearted, the tear-streaked, to join the Savior in lifting them out of the ash heap, wiping their tears, restoring them to hope—even as we are being consoled by the One who cares for us.[15] We will be people who refuse to cling to power,

---

14. Rev 21:1–4, 22–27.
15. 1 Pet 5:7.

who refuse the inhumanity of domination, and who refuse indifference or hopelessness, instead walking in the light of the Lamb, choosing the path of self-giving love, rejoicing in the One who is making all things new.[16] We will be people unwilling to be overcome by feelings of futility in the face of the way things are, instead moving with all we are and have towards that city whose gates are never shut and whose righteousness shines like the sun.

Prayer is what keeps all that from becoming a utopian daydream. It is easy to become cynical, given the state of our familiar politics. In the shadow of politicians who say one thing and do another, whose primary motivations seem to be re-election rather than renewal, profit over prophecy, grabbing at power over the honor and glory of a crucified God, we could give up on hoping in anything "political." Prayer is what cuts through cynicism, holds our doubts without giving them undue weight, and empowers us not only to contemplate another way but to confirm it with our lives.[17] Prayer is what enables us to organize our passions and commitments, our time and our stuff, around the One who is heaven-bent on being for us Wonderful Counselor, Mighty God, Everlasting Father, Prince of Peace.[18]

Prayer Is Presence, Not Transaction

Prayer helps us organize our lives around the will and way of God because prayer is primarily an act of presence. It is loving attention to the One who made us and loves us beyond measure. Too often we reduce prayer to asking for things. It is right and good to ask God for things, to cast our cares on the One who cares for us.[19] Jesus himself teaches us to ask for things, to pray for our daily bread. He tells us that asking is key to receiving.[20] St. Paul is always telling folks not to worry about things, but to pray about them. But prayer is so much more than asking: it's rejoicing in the Lord.[21] It's glorifying God.[22] It's crying out in pain and frustration and worse.[23] It's being

16. Rev 21:5.
17. Phil 1:7; Col 1:29.
18. Isa 9:6.
19. 1 Pet 5:7.
20. Matt 5:7.
21. Phil 4:4.
22. Matt 6:9.
23. A significant proportion of the Psalms either contain, or are entirely, lament. These biblical prayers invite us not only to ask for God's saving help, but also to voice our deepest agonies.

still, quieting our souls, like a child in the arms of her mother.[24] The wild expanse of the Psalms, the prayerbook of the Bible, shows us that prayer is mostly the way in which we bring our whole selves into the presence of God, not hiding anything. Prayer is primarily presence.

It's telling that, at least once, St. Paul is clear that he understands there to be a difference between prayer as a practice and the varied elements that might make up our devotional life: "Do not be anxious about anything, but in everything by prayer and supplication with thanksgiving let your requests be made known to God."[25] For many of us, supplication and thanksgiving might be the sum total of our prayer practice. And those things are good and necessary. It is relatively simple to come up with things to ask for. If we are paying any attention at all to the world around, supplication will come naturally. There is much to ask for. And if we are paying any attention at all to the world around, thanksgiving will flow from us. The bigness and smallness of things, the wonder of life when there could be nothing, the gift of friendship, the beauty of creation—there is much to be grateful for. But, by separating those prayerful elements from the *act* of prayer, Paul seems to be making a subtle point that prayer is more. Prayer is the way that we learn how to ask and give thanks in ways appropriate to the ways and means of God. It's growing in relationship with the God who is relentlessly relational. We must not allow prayer to become transactional—something we do so that God will give us what we want, or simply to keep ourselves in God's good books.

One of the challenges of letting prayer be the way to relationship with God is that relationships are not always all that exciting. It can be exciting to anticipate moments of spiritual ecstasy or the harnessing of a power well beyond what we can muster up. It can be thrilling to look forward to the liminal space of a retreat center, or a raucous prayer service, expecting an extraordinary divine encounter. And maybe there's nothing wrong with creating the conditions for those "special" moments, but they cannot sustain a life of prayer. As Sarah Coakley puts it, "We only have to spend about five seconds in silence before we're thinking, 'This is boring. Why don't I go do something more exciting?'"[26] The trouble is, excitement and novelty are lousy foundations on which to build any relationship. Most of us know that

---

24. Ps 131.
25. Phil 4:6.
26. Coakley and Koh, "Divine Propulsion."

our most cherished relationships, the ones with the people we trust with our lives, who lighten our hearts whenever they are around, are the ones in which we can sit quietly on the couch and let nothing particular happen. It doesn't mean that there are not moments of passion or deep joy, seasons of excitement and adventures that awaken feelings that might get ignored in the ups and downs of everyday life. But the gift of deep relationships is not in excitement, but in solidity. Jesus's invitation is not to spiritual thrill-seeking, but to build a home on his solid foundation, to construct a life in which every moment, even the most mundane ones, might be building blocks for heaven's kingdom.[27]

Understanding prayer as presence—unity with God wherever we are and whatever we're doing—gives us space to imagine that St. Paul's instruction to do *everything* we do in the name of Jesus, to the glory of God is actually possible.[28] Developing an awareness of God's presence in the ordinary, and even the boring, keeps us from reducing our spiritual lives to a kind of abstract theology: something we believe but don't do. Prayer as presence allows that there is nothing in or around us that is inconsequential to God, and there is nothing we do that has nothing to do with God. It is so easy to live fragmented and fractured lives, everything compartmentalized so that what happens at the office bears no resemblance to what happens at home, our worship and our free time are unrelated, how we are with our friends may bear no relation to how we are with our family. Such disjointedness makes us good consumers, our various identities relentlessly catered to by numberless providers of services and stuff. Unfortunately, we will inevitably find ourselves reduced to mismatched pieces rather than living in the wholeness for which we are made. Disintegration is a demonic strategy for keeping us clinging to things that do not satisfy and limiting our capacity to attend to things as they actually are.

One way to counteract disintegration is paying holy attention—which is to say, prayerful attention—to the people we find ourselves with, and places we find ourselves in. Learning to recognize each person and space, each element of creation, each moment and breath as bound up in the drama of God's salvation keeps us from manically seeking the satisfactions of our deepest longings anywhere other than in the stuff that makes up our everyday lives. Eugene Peterson puts it this way:

---

27. Matt 7:24–27.
28. 1 Cor 10:31; Col 3:17.

> Comprehension of the invisible begins in the visible. Praying to God begins by looking at a tree. The deepest relationship of which we are capable has its origin in the everyday experience of taking a good look at what is in everybody's backyard. We are not launched into the life of prayer by making ourselves more heavenly, but by immersing ourselves in the earthy: not by formulating abstractions such as goodness, beauty, or even God, but by attending to trees and tree toads, mountains and mosquitoes.... Abstraction is an enemy to prayer.[29]

Cultivating prayerful presence means embracing the dull moments, the run-of-the-mill "backyard" stuff, as instances where divinity is glad to be. It means showing up to devotional times when we don't much feel like it and listening for the Spirit's still small voice when everything feels like spiritual white noise. It means patience and forbearance and sticktoitiveness, things not widely celebrated in much of Western culture. Pastor Rich Villodas, when teaching on prayer, invites us to "embrace boredom," which allows us to be present even when we're not entertained.[30] To embrace the boredom of prayer, which makes up the bulk of most people's prayer life, is actually to enter into the breathtaking wonder that the God our souls thirst for does not require us to work ourselves into a frenzy, or create the ideal spiritual space, or come up with the most expressive words, but is simply glad to be with us, doing nothing in particular. When we understand that, then we're on to something.

Prayerful presence is not always exciting, and neither is it always easy. Like any relationship, there is work, intention, effort, and a willingness to seek the good of the other, whether we feel like it or not. And in the vicissitudes of life, we may not feel like it more often than we're comfortable admitting. The Psalms as a whole confront us with the fact that a faithful relationship with our God is not always a walk in the garden. Sometimes it's frustration and anger, loss and fear; sometimes the best we can muster is a tense hopefulness that maybe God will listen this time. "Many are the afflictions of the righteous," and sometimes we just want to know why. Psalm 34 is determined in confidence that the Lord answers, saves, heals, and is near to the brokenhearted. But its location within the whole psalter puts us in contact with other prayers and pray-ers that are not so confident. And our location among the Body of Christ, parts of which are praying on

---

29. Peterson, *Answering God*, 27.
30. Villodas, *Deeply Formed Life*.

cancer wards and in homeless shelters, in war zones and food bank lines and prison cells, places that may well seem Godforsaken, puts us in contact with those praying in doubt and pain. We will come to "holy heartbreak" shortly, as a signpost for Christian strangeness. Suffice it to say here that there are days and weeks and seasons and years when "blessing the Lord at all times" feels more aspirational than possible.

Yet, even the prayers that lead us in lament point us to the One who refuses to stay away until the conditions are right but gets down in the ash heap of ruined lives and best-laid plans, to lift us up.[31] If any God has forsaken us, he is still "my God." And even when it feels trite, the tireless truth holds that God's faithfulness to us is not in proportion to our faithfulness to him, and our cries of help will be heard. Even when it isn't easy, our hope is still in the name of the Lord. What's more, experience tells us that there are no relationships that flourish over years that do not have stretches that feel more like work than pleasure. While times of trial can wither some relationships, fallow and fertilizing seasons often make others stronger. I wonder if that's why St. James can say something as discordant to our ears as "whenever you face trials of any kind, consider it nothing but joy, because you know that the testing of your faith produces endurance; and let endurance have its full effect, so that you may be mature and complete, lacking in nothing."[32] James might have failed Pastoral Care 101, but perhaps, especially on this side of the resurrection, he's pointing us to the promise that wrestling a blessing out of God is sometimes the way to a new day, a possibility we'd never imagined, an opportunity to draw near to the One who has drawn eternally near to us.

All of our prayers take shape between two images of intimacy. The first is in our past: the glory of God strolling in the garden, "at the time of the evening breeze"[33] simply looking to be with Adam and Eve, to enjoy their company, to know them "naked and unashamed."[34] God still wants that, wants leisurely time with us, our whole selves. God still calls us into that kind of intimate presence. And then: in our future, the day when that intimacy is fully restored, the total presence that St. John sees on his knees in prayer, on Patmos. All of our prayer happens between the garden of Eden and the city of God. Every prayer grows out of that primordial intimacy and towards that

31. Ps 113:7.
32. Jas 1:2–3.
33. Gen 3:8.
34. Gen 2:25.

day when it will be total. To know and practice prayer as presence is to draw past and future into this time, this place, with these people.

Prayer Is a Way of Life

Whatever St. Paul means by "praying without ceasing"[35] it cannot be that he expects us all to live lives of cloistered devotion, cut off from the world. Even if he could have anticipated that some people would be called to such an extreme vocation in the service of the church, it's hard to imagine the itinerant evangelist sitting still for too long. Instead, he must mean something closer to David's learning to "bless the Lord at all times." To say that prayer is a way of life means allowing the formation of prayer that shapes us towards God's future, and the reciprocal presence experienced in prayer as we open ourselves to God and God offers himself to us, to then move us into the world to participate in what God is already doing.

There's a story early in the Gospel of Mark that points us to a prayerful way of life. Mark tells us:

> In the morning, while it was still very dark, [Jesus] got up and went out to a deserted place, and there he prayed. And Simon and his companions hunted for him. When they found him, they said to him, "Everyone is searching for you." He answered, "Let us go on to the neighboring towns, so that I may proclaim the message there also; for that is what I came out to do." And he went throughout Galilee proclaiming the message in their synagogues and casting out demons.

This early morning prayer time in the wilderness follows an evening of mass healings, in the wake of Jesus calling his first disciples. From the first days of Jesus's ministry, we see this pattern of prayer and action, action and prayer, outward movement in holy tension with prayerful retreat. It's important that Mark tells us Jesus went into a deserted place. The Greek is *eremōn*, sometimes also translated as "wilderness." Biblically speaking the *eremōn* is the place of formation. It's the wilderness through which God brings Israel, teaching them what it means to walk in freedom, as God's people, after generations of enslavement in Egypt. It's the *eremōn* in which Jesus is tempted, facing down the devil's wiles in the company of beasts and angels. So, this prayer is not simply a quiet time away, before the day's work.

---

35. 1 Thess 5:16.

This is a willful entering into a place of formation, submission to the ways and means of the One he calls Father.

It is also an act of presence, away from the noise and distraction of the crowds, apart from the work that's to be done. We might allow ourselves to imagine that the sparseness of the telling is an indication that this was not one of the "I think I'll go walk on water now" or "he was lit up like the sun" prayer times.[36] Might we even imagine that Jesus rolled out of bed before sunrise, not much interested in doing so, and went out to embrace sleepy boredom in the presence of his Father? Whatever the case, there, he prayed. He was present to the One who calls him Beloved, whose Spirit fills and animates, forms, and empowers.[37]

Then, like for any of us, the day bursts into the quiet. Simon and the others track him down, with local gossip and fresh demands—*everyone is looking for you*. It would not be unreasonable to think that Jesus might have scolded them for interrupting his prayer time. Can't they see he's having a moment? But there is no great sigh of annoyance or sharpness in his response. The day has arrived, and there is work to do. And here we come to another important moment in the story: it seems to me that there could be good strategy in setting up shop here in Capernaum. It won't take long for word to spread to the surrounding villages of his healing ministry. They could get a little sign, make themselves at home, and have everyone come to them. After all, already, "everyone is looking for you." It's hard to not to imagine that is what Peter had in mind. They are in his hometown, the outburst of healings happened at his door, it's beginning to look like a good call to drop his fishing nets and follow this rabbi.

But, coming out of prayer, Jesus is clear about what's next. He will not be setting up shop in Capernaum, even if that's the safe bet. He must go to the other villages, *because that is what I came out to do*. The formation and presence of prayer nurtures clarity of purpose. He is embodying the love of God for this world that is on the move, coming towards us, not waiting for us to come find him. This is the prodigal father who, while his son was still a long way off, runs to meet him.[38] The formation and presence of prayer propels Jesus into the work that God is about. He sets out proclaiming good news and casting out demons, the Son participating in the favor, the healing, the redemption, and release of the Father.

36. Mark 6:45–52; Mark 9:3.
37. Mark 1:11.
38. Luke 15:20.

Jesus models prayer as a way of life, prayer lived out, embodied, given voice and action in the world. There is a tendency in the church for people to believe that we need to make a choice between contemplation and action, between the quiet discipline of prayer, in the dark, unseen, and the active outworking of our faith. It's a false choice. It's nonsense. The reality is that our apprenticeship to Jesus demands both. We need *erēmon* formation in the way of God's freedom. We need leisurely submission to the One who calls us beloved, so that we can learn to receive that identity over any other. We need times of simple openness to the Holy Spirit who mingles and testifies with our spirits that we are children of God, the Spirit who prays for us when we don't have the words.[39] And we need to feel the easy burden of God's call into the world to give shape and witness to what we have come to know in God's presence: that God so loves this world, that God is making all things new, and there is nothing in heaven, earth, or hell that will separate us from the love of God in Christ Jesus our Lord.

Prayer as a way of life means allowing God to form us, so that wherever we go and whatever we do, we are ready to lock step with the Spirit, as agents of God's redeeming love in the office, at home, with friends and family, in the checkout line, the classroom, and the boardroom, on the bus or on the beach; there is nowhere that is ceded to anything less than the grace of God and God's oncoming kingdom. It's a lifetime of learning to say, with the One we follow, "I can only do what I see the Father doing," with everything we've got.[40]

---

39. Rom 8:26–27.
40. John 5:19.

Signpost 3

Incarnation

Salvation as Christians know it is not merely the declaration to sinners that all is forgiven; it is the living out of forgiveness in the presence of sin—the "with-ness" and work of grace in the midst of regular, sinful human life.[1]

Look to him, and be radiant.... O taste and see that the LORD is good.

PSALM 34:5A, 8A

Incarnation Is Weird

THE CHRISTIAN DOCTRINE OF the incarnation—the affirmation that the God of heaven and earth, who made mountains and molehills, quarks and quasars, entered into the world through the womb of a no-name young woman from a backwoods town, grew up the son of a laborer, and lived a short life and had a much shorter ministry, wandering a tiny plot of land on the far edge of the Roman Empire, until the powers that be killed him, after which he was raised from the dead and ascended to the throne of heaven—is weird. Its weirdness is one of the reasons many of us think it's true. If we were going to come up with a way for God to do "God things," this would be nowhere near the top of the list of options. Although apologetics, the practice of defending religious belief on the basis of reason and

---

1. Rowe, *Leading Christian Communities*, 129.

rational argument, has its place, I contend that the church would do well to re-embrace the absolute unreasonableness of the way God seems to do what God wants to do. We have not been particularly well-served by taming the basic claims of our faith, conforming them to the ways that we like to do things and trying to make them perfectly understandable. Because they are not. Plus, if God only does things that we can understand and accept intellectually, how boring is that? Don't we want a God who can exceed our expectations?

This is not the place to do a deep dive into Nicaean Orthodoxy, nor am I interested here in getting too deep into the weeds of two thousand years of theological debate.[2] Partly because that can often help us avoid the implications of the things we argue about. It is curiously easy when talking about incarnation—literally *embodiment*—to spiral off into abstractions, because there's safety in that. It often results in a sort of superhuman Jesus, who floats just above the ground, which is to say that he only bears a passing resemblance to the rest of us mere mortals. And when that happens, who and how Jesus is has precious little to do with our everyday lives. "We're only human" becomes an excuse to sidestep the challenge of Christian discipleship, instead of the very fact that draws us into living relationship with God. The claim of incarnation is not that God, in Christ, sort of got mixed up with us; rather the claim of incarnation is that the Word who was with God and was God from the beginning took on flesh and moved into the neighborhood, got right down in the dust with us.[3] He became like us, that we might become like him.[4]

The incarnation tells us profoundly important things (breathtaking things!) about who God is, and about how God is determined to fulfill the divine and saving promises made throughout the Hebrew Scriptures. First,

---

2. The Council of Nicaea was a coordinated effort, in 325, to arrive at a consensus around theological orthodoxy within Christendom, particularly concerning the divinity of Jesus and his eternal relationship with the Father. The Nicene Creed is generally understood to be the standard for Trinitarian orthodoxy.

3. John 1:1–18. I am increasingly compelled by scholars who argue that the Gospel of John is an earlier document than we have often thought. The dating itself is less interesting than the reality, bolstered by the earliest Christian writings in the New Testament, that, from the beginning, followers of Jesus recognized that in him the God they had known through Torah and the Prophets has done something altogether different. The doctrine of the Trinity may have taken another three hundred plus years to develop in the way that we know it today, but its reality has been there from the start.

4. This claim is made by Athanasius. See Christian History Institute, "Module 108: Athanasius."

it underscores the hope and promise that any salvation of us and this world will be accomplished in deeply intimate ways. God is not content to stay at a safe and heavenly distance, unsullied by humanity. Nor is God about to play at being human for a bit, like many of the ancient gods were wont to do, for some ulterior or self-serving reason. But this God is in the thick of it with us. This God will only be Emmanuel, God *with* us.[5] God will be our God, and we will be God's people.[6]

Secondly, the incarnation tells us that God is not simply interested in a spiritualized salvation. Life with God is not only about our souls; it's about our bodies, about all of creation. All of creation groans under the weight of sin and death,[7] and God's determination is to alleviate that groaning, to restore and make whole all that evil would destroy. Ours is a tangible salvation, a goodness we can "taste and see," just like David invites us to do in our Song for the Strange. Elsewhere he invites us to join in singing, "I believe that I shall see the goodness of God in the land of the living." Not, somewhere beyond this world, but the goodness of God will be found here. That the Word becomes flesh and lives among us confirms that God actually does so love *this* world, that God is willing to give everything for it. That is not a self-evident truth without the fullness of the incarnation.

That's a third thing: It matters that God loves us right to the grave and then through it. It is easy enough to imagine a benevolent deity when things are well, in the presence of beauty or the joys of love. It becomes rather more difficult to trust that God loves us when things go sideways, in the face of the death and destruction that plague our species and the planet, or when—by any objective human standards—we are just not all that lovable, when sin has its way in and through us. The first followers of the Way, trying to make sense of the world in the wake of Jesus's resurrection, came up against the staggering reality that God's love was infinitely wider, longer, higher, and deeper than they had understood. The tapestry of the gospel had to be stretched much further than had been previously imagined.[8] And it wasn't just that all of a sudden they had to figure out how to get gentiles into this new, distinctly Jewish movement, which was one issue.[9] They also had to contend with the idea that "while *we* were still sinners Christ died

---

5. Isa 7:14; Matt 1:23.
6. Gen 17:1; Exod 6:7; Lev 26:12; Jer 24:27; Ezek 34:24.
7. Rom 8:22.
8. Jennings, *Acts*, 143.
9. Acts 15.

for *us*."¹⁰ Or that, "in [Jesus] all the fullness of God was pleased to dwell, and through him God was pleased to reconcile to himself *all things*, whether on earth or in heaven, by making peace through the blood of his cross."¹¹ Irrespective of our preferred atonement theories, there is something astonishing about the God who looks like Jesus, not only in life, but in death. Who in the world is this God, who self-empties for humanity, long before we think to do anything for God? Who in the world is this God who is willing to dwell fully in the body of a Galilean laborer, and even more is *pleased* to reconcile all things in heaven and earth by his own blood? Who is this God who is kind to the ungrateful and the wicked?¹² Mercifully: the God we've got.

There is surely much more to say about the incarnation as a doctrine, a foundational piece of Christian faith. But for our purposes, it is enough to let our imaginations run with the implications of the Word made flesh. Because what is every bit as astonishing is that in the wake of Christ's ascension the fact of the incarnation has significant implications for his apprentices on earth.¹³ The power and presence of God, fully found in Jesus, is now pleased to be found in his followers. That, I think we must admit, is just as weird. Maybe more so. It is both beautiful and unnerving to know that Jesus trusts us with his ministry, that the Holy Spirit is pleased to testify with our spirits that we too are children of God, which means that we too are those learning to do nothing more or less than what we see God doing in Jesus. Among the Gospel writers, John is the most explicit about this. In his Gospel, we overhear Jesus telling the disciples that *anyone* who believes in him will do what he does *and even greater things*.¹⁴ We hear Jesus insist that we can be one with him and each other as he and the Father are one.¹⁵ In the upper room, on the first Easter evening he says, astonishingly: "As the Father sent me, *so I send you*."¹⁶

All this means that while the incarnation of Jesus, as the Word made flesh, is a unique historical reality, Christian faith is a necessarily incarnate

---

10. Rom 5:8, italics added.
11. Col 3:19–20, italics added.
12. Luke 6:35.
13. Luke 24:50–51; Acts 1:9. For some thoughts on the ascension, see Miller, *Witnesses of These Things*, ch. 5.
14. John 14:12.
15. John 17:21–22.
16. John 20:21, italics added.

faith. There is nothing in Scripture or theology that can be understood as both Christian and unlived. The incarnation makes clear that God's redeeming work only happens on the ground, in the particularities of every human life, the specificity of every earthly place, the unrepeatability of every human interaction. Perhaps what's most astonishing about John's proclamation that the Word, the eternal *logos*, took on flesh and lived among us, is that what was general, universal, ethereal (*logos*) becomes local, particular, and specific. This is how God's salvation is revealed, not as a universal and general truth, but in One who gets close enough to touch, whose ministry involves bread, wine, breath, and saliva. And so, those of us who follow him deal in things every bit as tangible.

I confess I have never been quite sure how to understand Jesus's claim that we who believe in him will do what he does and even greater things. I feel like I, and every believer I know, falls a fair way short of the wild things we see in Jesus, the world changing embodiment of God's grace and love. But I am also inclined to wonder if Jesus doesn't take us a little more seriously than we do ourselves, if Jesus recognizes the wonder and miracle of every life in a way we rarely do. Too often, among believers, I think we see a hesitancy, an unwillingness to accept that these little lives, these frail bodies, this ordinary circumstance, all the things that make up our everyday experience are sufficient to bear witness to the extravagant goodness of God, the glory of God, the redemption and renewal of all things. We just don't think we are quite up for it, quite enough to be like Jesus and do what he does. Unfortunately, that may be closer to obstinance than humility.

I have often wondered why we do not have more information about Jesus as a kid. I want stories about fourteen-year-old Jesus. What was Jesus like in the throes of puberty? It feels a touch sacrilegious to think about Jesus's voice cracking and his awkward attempts to talk to crushes. But the Scriptures are insistent that he experienced everything that we do.[17] He knows what it's like to be a human, in all our mess and wonder. The truth is that most ancient biographies had little to say about their subjects' childhood.[18] Childhood experiences were not worth mentioning. But what if that is part of the point? What if the reason we know so little about Jesus's life before his ministry is that it was mostly unremarkable? And what if that means not that the incarnation is unremarkable, but that our lives are wildly more remarkable than we imagine? If Jesus's early life was more or

---

17. Heb 4:15.
18. Raphael, *Jew Among Romans*, 28.

less like every other kid in first-century Nazareth, is that not amazing in its own right? It would tell us that the normal, everyday stuff of our life is a place the fullness of God is pleased to dwell. There are some pseudonymous, much later biographies that try to fill in the blanks, complete with miracles and acts appropriate to God in the flesh. But the church quickly disregarded them, recognizing that they were incoherent with the earliest testimonies to Jesus's life and work. But that some folks tried to make Jesus more interesting suggests that it has always been a little uncomfortable to know that Jesus was—and, heaven help us, is—more like us than we might have been led to believe. Because that is not a diminishment of Jesus, but an invitation to us to fully embrace the wild wonder that here and now we too are children of God, made in God's image, fit to reflect and reveal the goodness of God with all we've got and wherever we are.

As David leads us in prayer, not only in Ps 34, but at every turn, there is never the sense that we're dealing with anything less than what is right in front of us. On the ground, in the lives we actually have, is where the Lord, whose praise we get to have continually in our mouths, is found. Ours is a faith to be tasted and seen, a faith deepened by simple, physical things like sharing a meal or taking a walk, receiving the Eucharist or meditating on a painting. The more our senses come alive, the more deeply we know the God who made them.

Incarnation Is Political

The incarnation makes clear that God's determination to redeem this world is a tangible reality, which stretches beyond our personal lives and circumstances. An incarnate faith has every bit as much to do with systemic salvation, the redemption of all things in heaven and earth, as with our immortal souls; it has to do with the ways in which we live and move and have our being with one another, with our neighbors, with all of creation. The invitation to trust that we will "see the goodness of God in the land of the living"[19] compels us to live towards that day when God's goodness will fill the whole earth, when every tear is wiped away and every hungry belly filled, and all things are made new, which means that the incarnation is unavoidably political.

To take the incarnation seriously is to alter the way that we organize ourselves. It means concerning ourselves with the things that Jesus

---

19. Ps 27:13.

concerned himself with: good news for the poor, release for those who are bound, fresh sight for those blinded to any possibility other than the way things are, freedom for the oppressed, the proclamation of Jubilee—the radical reorganizing of society for the health and flourishing of people and creation.[20] Needless to say, that is not the sort of politics that Christians have become known for in the popular secular imagination. By those outside the church, we are more likely to be associated with those committed to the status quo, clambering after power, exerting control, embroiled in the maintenance of the kingdoms of the world, rather than pursuing the kingdom of heaven.

This reputation is lamentable, principally because a cursory tour of the Gospels makes clear that from the earliest days of the Jesus movement, the church collectively understood itself as an alternative system to those that governed the world around. From the get-go, the incarnation is clearly an affront to the way things are. We hear that when the Magi showed up in Jerusalem, looking for the child who had been born King of the Jews, Herod—the Roman puppet king—was terrified, and all Jerusalem with him.[21] One guesses that "all Jerusalem" refers to the movers and shakers, whose opinion and concern mattered. Matthew is not explicit about why exactly Herod is so disturbed, but the arrival of a rival king is never a good situation for those who want to hold on to power. What's more, in the shadow of the Roman Empire, new kings were not celebrated. The kind of political turmoil that attended a change in the crown was bound to get the attention of Rome and its violent determination to keep peace by eliminating any disturbances. If that meant taking out a city to set an example, so be it. Herod was desperate and ruthless when it came to maintaining his regal position, even if his authority was dependent on Rome's ongoing support. Those determined to cling to power tend to panic at the least threat to their standing. Even an improbable king, born among livestock in nowheresville, far from the centers of control, is enough to send those committed to the current order of things spiralling into violent anxiety.

In Luke's Gospel we see a similar tension between Jesus and the powers that be. Perhaps the most telling moment is when Jesus is facing down the devil's temptations in the wilderness. The second temptation is to take control of all the kingdoms of the world, over which Satan has authority—so he claims. All that's required is for Jesus to sell out and worship the

20. Luke 4:16–20.
21. Matt 2:3.

tempter, and it can all be his.²² He can shape the world in whatever way he sees fit, if he'll just sacrifice his identity as Beloved of God, the Son in whom the Father is well pleased, and commit himself to another. It may be a bit on the nose to consider the kingdoms of the world as invariably under demonic control. But the moment, Jesus's resistance to the temptation, makes clear that the familiar ways of seizing control by any means necessary will be very different from the way that Jesus will be King. In the kingdom of heaven, the means and the ends need to match up.

Another poignant moment happens later in the story, when we see the Jerusalem power brokers aligned to put an end to the upstart rabbi from Nazareth. We're told that following Jesus's arrest, and anticipating his crucifixion, "that day Herod and Pilate became friends—before this they had been enemies."²³ Even if we take the critics seriously, and allow that there may a bit of artistic license taken here and throughout the Gospels, it tells us something important about what the earliest followers of the Way of Jesus thought was happening. They had been caught up with the One who had all the power in the world but chose to let it all go, emptying himself for love's sake.²⁴ They had come to see that the cross was not the end of another failed prophet, but the means by which the God of resurrection has rendered the temper tantrums of worldly power utterly foolish.²⁵ They were learning to pray, "Thy kingdom (not ours, or Herod's, or Caesar's) come; Thy will (not ours, or Herod's, or Caesar's) be done, on earth as in heaven." And not only to pray it, but to organize their lives in such a way that the fullness of God that entered the world in Jesus Christ might be made known every bit as clearly in the ways that they lived with each other and their neighbors.

For many, the most famous indication that the incarnate Way of Jesus is unavoidably political is the Great Commission, Matt 28:16–20. There we hear that all authority in heaven and earth has been given to the risen Christ. The kings of the world can rant and rave all they want, but the Prince of Peace sits on heaven's throne forever. That is the confidence and conviction by which the church determines its politics. Our posture in the world is to be a reflection of the One who gave up divine power, humbling himself even to the point of death on a cross, and *therefore* (not in spite of that fact), his name is the name above every other. He is worthy to be

22. Luke 4:5–7.
23. Luke 23:12.
24. Phil 2:5–11.
25. Col 2:15.

followed not because he wrested power away for himself, but because of his determination to serve the world in love. All authority in heaven and earth is given to him because he is the One who can be trusted to wield that authority in justice and righteousness, the One whose default is forgiveness, mercy, and peace. And that's why those who would walk in his way, who trust him as savior and redeemer, are perfectly free to do whatever we do in the name and Way of Jesus, to the glory of God. Anything that cannot be done under the conditions of Jesus's lordship is fruitless, not worth our time and energy, even if it seems more efficient than the means of grace or garners the admiration of the world.

Along with the narrative framework of the Gospels, the linguistic choices of early Christian witnesses shape an imagination for the ways in which our politics go against the grain of the way things are. Words we use all the time in church, like "Savior," "Lord," "Redeemer," are all titles familiar to folks in the first century, because they were applied to Caesar.[26] Applying them to Jesus is a bold statement about what is really going on. When, in John's Gospel, Jesus promises his disciples that his gift is peace, and not in the way that the world gives peace,[27] he intentionally sets his way against the so-called *Pax Romana*—peace that comes at the end of a sword and can be quickly taken away. Even "authority" would have been understood to be granted by Rome, but Jesus's authority comes not from the allegiance to the emperor, but from God. So, when Peter and John are dragged in front of the Jerusalem council and told to knock it off with all the Jesus talk, they answer, "Whether it is right in God's sight to listen to you rather than to God, you must judge; for we cannot keep from speaking about what we have seen and heard."[28] This is not just rebelliousness. The disciples are learning to live within the tension of the world that is and the world that is coming. In the Way of Jesus, all earthly authority is relativized, secondary to the new reality that constitutes the in-breaking of heaven's kingdom. They are learning to work out their commitment to Jesus, crucified, risen, and reigning, in a way that turns the world upside down.[29]

In its own way, Ps 34 shapes a political imagination coherent with the will and way of God. As David leads us in the conviction that the "eyes of the Lord are on the righteous," and "the face of the Lord is against evildoers"

---

26. Claiborne and Haw, *Jesus for President*, 67–68.
27. John 14:27.
28. Acts 4:19–20.
29. Acts 17:7.

he guides us towards a way of living in the world that makes clear that the promises of God are sure. David forces us to attend to the ways that our lives align with the ways and means of God in the world, whoever we are with and wherever we find ourselves. Righteousness and evil are not simply spiritual realities; they are lived ones. Righteousness is necessarily relational—it is to be in right relationship with God, our true selves, each other, and creation. We cannot pursue righteousness in theory; it is not an abstract principle. It has everything to do with the way that we are in the world. It is the way we interact with, care for, and seek the flourishing of our communities. Biblically, righteousness and care for the least and the lost are absolutely entwined.

Likewise, evil is consistently relational, worked out in the details of our lives and between people. The prophets rail against those who hold power in such a way that it crushes others. The Word of the Lord is regularly raised against those who trample others in pursuit of vainglory. Evil is relentlessly interpersonal while simultaneously depersonalizing. Evil does its most effective work when we are convinced to disregard the humanity of others, exalting ourselves at the expense of the flourishing of those within our sphere of influence, irrespective of the size of that sphere. Political evil is not restricted to those who obviously hold power, or any one political persuasion. Every one of us is capable of dehumanizing evil. And every one of us is capable of wondrous righteousness. In every interaction we have the power to build up or tear down, nurture or injure, move towards justice or seek our own elevation.

Incarnation Is Presence, Not (Just) Preaching

Somehow, we have allowed the name of Jesus to be associated with clamoring after power and wealth, indifference to the poor and marginalized, and the destruction of the planet. It is surreal and depressing to think that the name of Jesus is so regularly invoked—at least in the popular imagination, even if not in most Christian communities around the globe—not to upend the way things are but to justify them. Or that to preach the gospel, not only as a proclamation of the word of God, but a living witness to our conviction that it's true, is increasingly considered a left-wing conspiracy against the kingdom of heaven.[30]

---

30. See, for instance, Chappell, "Woke Agenda and Its Influence on Churches and Colleges." In this article, Dr. Paul Chappell, senior pastor of Lancaster Baptist Church

While a prooftexting competition may garner some points for those who insist that salvation only comes through the hearing of God's word,[31] to suggest that preaching the gospel is the exclusive requirement of followers of Jesus while social justice is optional or somewhat beneficial is shortsighted to the point of absurdity. St. Paul himself equates the "defense *and* confirmation" of the gospel, proclamation and practice of the good news.[32] Jesus's ministry consistently combines preaching and teaching with healings and practical service for those who are "harassed and helpless."[33] The commands to love God *and* neighbor are indistinguishable for those committed to following Jesus towards the world as God would have it. The two are inseparable. St. James makes it as clear as anybody, that you gotta feed and clothe the hungry and naked, not just talk about it, or spiritualize it.

> What good is it, my brothers and sisters, if you say that you have faith but do not have works? Can faith save you? If a brother or sister is naked and lacks daily food, and one of you says to them, "Go in peace; keep warm and eat your fill," and yet does not supply their bodily needs, what is the good of that? So faith without works is dead.
>
> But some will say, "You have faith and I have works." Show me your faith apart from your works, and I by my works will show you my faith. . . . For just as the body without the spirit is dead, so faith without works is also dead.[34]

One could assume that the hearing of the word and believing it should so radically change a person that they cannot help but work for justice, cannot help but take seriously the humanity of everyone they meet.[35] To be in Christ is to be a new creation, after all.[36] And yet, even so committed a believer as Paul can acknowledge the tension between what he knows he ought to do and what he does. "I do not understand my own actions. For

---

and president of West Coast Baptist College, contends that even someone like Tim Keller, evangelical pastor and Christian apologist, has missed the mark of orthodoxy by equating in importance the proclamation of the gospel and its outworking for the sake of the common good.

31. Rom 10:17.
32. Phil 1:7, italics added.
33. Matt 9:36.
34. Jas 2:14–18, 26.
35. As Dr. Chappell does. See n30.
36. 2 Cor 5:17.

I do not do what I want, but I do the very thing I hate."[37] Even those of us who strive after the Way of Jesus can find ourselves at odds with the very way that we long for. Thus, part of following Jesus has to be the understanding that in one sense we are "saved" (forgiven of sin, reconciled to God, experiencing the grace of the One who makes all things new, receiving the proclamation of the Gospel); we are also "being saved."[38] That is, we are constantly growing in our apprenticeship to Jesus, until that day, on the other side of this life, when we are one with him. And that requires sustained attention to the way that our daily life, the way that we are present in the world, foreshadows that day.

Another way to say it is that Christian faith has more to do with presence than preaching. Of course, proclamation matters.[39] But proclamation without practice is pointless; we need orthopraxy, not just orthodoxy. What's more, this is about more than the sorts of things we tend to associate with social justice. It's not about less, but to grow in the Way of Jesus means understanding that every interaction is a space for the confirmation of the gospel. It would be foolish to imagine that we can change the broken systems of the world while failing to take seriously the people right in front of us and the places all around us. And that means that the church should be training ground for learning how to live in ways that reveal the hope that is ours, with each other. The church is meant to be a community in which we learn how to be present to one another, in all our mess and glory, learning to know that each of us is someone in whom the Holy Spirit is pleased to dwell; each one of us is someone made to be filled with all the fullness of God—whether it looks that way or not.

Willie James Jennings puts it like this: "The single greatest challenge for disciples of Jesus is to imagine and then enact actual life together, life that interpenetrates, weaves together, and joins to the bone."[40] Perhaps the single greatest obstacle to that kind of community is distraction—whether by the "cares of the world and the lure of wealth,"[41] the myriad ways that our cultures compel us to obsess over our standing and value, or the ubiquity of screens, and the sensory overload so regularly inflicted upon us by the noise of the world.

37. Rom 7:15.
38. Acts 2:47; 1 Cor 1:18.
39. Rom 10:14.
40. Jennings, *Acts*, 145.
41. Mark 4:19.

These days, we live in what is primarily an "attention economy."[42] Algorithms on our smartphones that are only designed to keep us staring into the screen for the profit of someone else, relentless advertisements that are increasingly invasive—every blank space an opportunity to point our attention towards something we might like to own or use or become—talking heads eager to entice us to their products or perspectives, all of it is so much noise that erodes our capacity for actual life together. There may be other things that get in the way of community that "joins to the bone," but the relentless demands on our attention and the ease of distraction must be recognized as a primary hindrance to deep investment in the images of God we find ourselves among.[43] Instead of growing in unity and love, we find ourselves fragmented and distracted, rarely "where our bodies are."[44] In the midst of so many options and demands, we are not only unable to attend to our neighbors, but we are also hindered in our ability to receive the gifts of the Spirit. Love, joy, peace, patience, kindness, generosity, faithfulness, gentleness, and self-control can get no grip on us, because those things can only be worked out and enjoyed with interpersonal intention.[45] In other words, they must be *incarnated*. That feels increasingly difficult and necessary. One need not be an expert in cultural studies to know that our current context is much more conducive to lust, momentary happiness, resignation, urgency, self-centeredness, self-protection, promiscuity (spiritual and otherwise), harshness, and self-indulgence—pale reflections or outright degradations of the things we are made for. This may have always been true, but modern technology has exacerbated the problem exponentially.

What are we to do under these conditions? The answer(s) may be complex, but at the very least we must strive to make our churches places in which we not only celebrate and proclaim the incarnation, but places in which we are learning to incarnate the hope that we have, the goodness of God that we have "seen with our eyes, looked at and touched with our hands, concerning the word of life."[46] Which means consciously creating opportunities for deep presence with one another and with God.

---

42. Crawford, *World Beyond*, 4.

43. Gen 1:27.

44. I am grateful to Andrew Root for this insight. At a lecture series given at the Vancouver School of Theology, he gathered us with the invitation to be where our bodies are.

45. Crawford, *World Beyond*, 7.

46. 1 John 1:1.

INCARNATION

I think of a church, planted by friends of mine who have a particular concern for those who have not been welcome in other churches because of their sexuality or gender expression, or who have been burnt out by toxic theologies that have more to do with free-market capitalism than the good news of Jesus Christ. Because they were focused on those for whom the church has been a place of failed and deeply fraught relationships, they were keen to structure their life and worship in ways that invited people to be deeply present both to the God who sees and loves them and one another. This meant doing things that were uncomfortable within their Anglican tradition when it came to things like Eucharist, making that celebration much more horizontal, choosing elements that allowed everyone to participate, and reducing or eliminating hierarchy whenever possible.[47] They had seasons in which they invited testimony, the practice of public faith-sharing, which is unusual in the mainline church, but which creates the kind of holy vulnerability that is necessary for deep relationships to flourish. They democratized worship leadership, inviting anyone—even those attending for the first time—to participate in readings or prayers or other liturgical elements, increasing the number of voices and bodies sharing in gospel proclamation.[48]

I fear that many congregations, irrespective of denominational affiliation, theological inclination, or worship style, tend to prize butts in pews as a metric of success over opportunities for deep, mutual presence. In an age of distraction, I am convinced that our souls long for communities that not only want us to be there—crowds do draw crowds, after all—but that make some demands on us that are appropriate to the gospel. We need communities that stretch and strengthen us to be with and for each other, in the way of the God who is eternally with and for us. If we will bear witness to the

---

47. For instance, they had a number of people in recovery, so—despite the bishop's protestations—they served juice along with wine. They also felt that it was important that everyone share in the same loaf, which meant sourcing the best gluten free bread they could find in the city, and then arranging schedules so that the bread could be procured each week. They received the elements in the round, each person passing the Body and Blood to the next, embodying their commitment to the priesthood of all believers.

48. Sadly, the community of St. Brigid's, in Vancouver, BC, found itself overwhelmed by the challenges of the COVID-19 pandemic and closed after ten years of ministry. Yet, their example and the healing that they facilitated and participated in continues to spark the holy imaginations of other communities committed to Christian community that "interpenetrates, weaves together, and joins to the bone." Their ministry is celebrated in the broader community, and the seeds planted during their decade of gospel witness continue to bear fruit, even as the community itself no longer meets.

One who is Emmanuel, doing the things he does, we must be willing to risk the kinds of intimacy and interdependence that he demonstrated in his earthly ministry, and continues in the ongoing gift of his Spirit. How that takes shape will be as diverse as the communities living it out. There are no cookie-cutter options for the kingdom of heaven; the Spirit blows where the Spirit pleases.[49] As with anything incarnate in the Way of Jesus, we must take seriously where we are and whom we're with. We can take inspiration from other communities—indeed we should. The beauty of the Body of Christ is in her many parts. But at the end of the day, our special attention and concern must be for the people and places that God has trusted us to care for. That means doing the work, which is sometimes a joy and sometimes a slog, to cultivate presence, as together we draw near to the God who has drawn near to us and live towards the world that God wants in this time and this place.

In all this, *place* really does matter. The redemption and reconciliation that God is working out in the world is about not only human souls, but all of creation. Part of caring for our human neighbors is deepening our care of our non-human neighbors. Being present to one is deepened by being present to the other. The systems and structures that lead to human flourishing are necessarily rooted in care for the world around us. Commitment to love and generosity, nurture and beauty, gentleness and grace, attention and presence—the stuff that makes human lives better—has to extend beyond the interpersonal.

One way to combat distraction, division, and disinterest is to cultivate wonder. It becomes less appealing to stare at our phones if we begin to take seriously the absolute miracle of the world around us. Consider the bigness and smallness of things, the complexity of life, the breathtaking reality of something when there could be nothing. Consider the unlikeliness of being alive in the world.[50] Apparently, the odds of being alive are so improbable as to be nothing short of miraculous. They are something like 1 in $10^{2,685,000}$.[51] That's a 10 followed by nearly 2.7 million zeros. Even the chances of our parents meeting, and successfully procreating, to make us, are 1 in 400 quadrillion.[52] The same is true for every person we meet, every

---

49. John 3:8.

50. I think Bill Bryson's *A Short History of Nearly Everything* is a wonderful invitation to wondering at the world around.

51. Mortal Atheist, "What Are the Odds of Being Alive?"

52. For reference, a million seconds is about 11.5 days. A billion seconds is nearly 32 years. A quadrillion seconds is 32 million years. Needless to say, you are spectacularly unlikely.

one we walk past without so much as a glance, every beggar and businessperson. Everyone. Everything. The whole world is shot through with that kind of incredible being. Seems like we would do well to enjoy it. And if we can develop sufficient wonder at the natural world, the plants and animals, oceans and rivers, mountains and prairies, wherever we are, it will become more and more difficult to treat the world as ours to exploit or live with indifference to its beauty.

A while back I started touching trees whenever I'm walking. And sometimes shrubs and flowers and grass. Usually just a gentle brush on the way past. Sometimes I stop with more intention. That may seem a bit weird, a little granola, perhaps I have been living in Cascadia too long. But this practice has helped me stay present, attentive to the world around me. And oddly, it has increased my awareness of life. The feel of bark and leaves brings me into the present, attentive to what's in front of me.[53] The moss that grows thick and fuzzy, the sap and berries, the bugs that make their home in and around it—turns out a tree is never just a tree; it's a whole universe of life. Perhaps that's why the psalmist says that when we're living well, attuned to God and the things God loves, fully ourselves as we are made to be, then we are like trees, planted by streams of water.[54] We are both nourished and nourishing, fruitful and flourishing, playing our little role in the wild wonder of life. That, it seems to me, is something like what it means to be present, incarnate, in the Way of Jesus.

All of that might be summed up by saying that the incarnate Way of Jesus is the way of love. Love not in theory, or as a feeling, but a practice—a decision to love God and neighbor, human and otherwise, with the stuff of our lives. When I think about incarnate love, the poem "Love Does That," by the Catholic monk and mystic Meister Eckhart:

> All day long a little burro labors, sometimes
> with heavy loads on her back and sometimes just with worries
> about things that only bother
> burros.

---

53. As a father of teenagers, I am often baffled by Gen Z slang. But I am fascinated by one phrase: "touch grass." This is directed at someone who has been inside on one or more screens for too long. I think it tells us something about the state of our culture that our youth have had to come up with a phrase to compel each other to experience the natural world.

54. Ps 1.

And worries, as we know, can be more exhausting
than physical labor.

Once in a while a kind monk comes
to her stable and brings
a pear, but more than that,

he looks into the burro's eyes and touches her ears

and for a few seconds the burro is free
and even seems to laugh,

because love does that.

Love frees.[55]

Incarnation Is a Way of Life

We have a tendency, nurtured by consumerism, to compartmentalize. We are better consumers when the various parts of our lives have sometimes only a passing relationship to each other. It is easier to sell us stuff when we embody different ways of being in different places and circumstances. It is better for the economy that we participate in, and often accept as an inevitability, if my priorities at work are different than my priorities at home, or with friends, or at church, because then my desires can be different in each place and satisfied by a wider variety of things. But a compartmentalized life is incoherent; it is draining and damaging, making us susceptible to temptation and manipulation. A compartmentalized life is unbiblical. Whether it renders us double-minded and fickle[56] or simply the kinds of people whose words and hearts, whose stated commitments and actions are at odds with each other, compartmentalization cuts against the wholeness for which we are made; it is not how we were created to be. When Jesus tells us to "be perfect, therefore, as your Father in heaven is perfect,"[57] he is not suggesting that we can be utterly without fault, but calling us to a kind of wholeness, unity of purpose, maturity, and wisdom. Not tossed around by every wind of doctrine, but deeply rooted, grounded in the ways and means of God.

---

55. Ladinsky, *Love Poems from God*, 108.
56. Jas 4:8.
57. Matt 5:48.

INCARNATION

As we consider that incarnation, the embodying of God's will and way in all we do, is not only a series of actions but an integrated way of life, we can begin by attending to something from the Cree language. Rev. Dr. Ray Aldred writes:

> The Nêhiyawak or Cree word for journeying is "pimâcihowin." The concept of living or journeying through the land is tied to the idea of health. Settler descendants might be surprised to discover that pimâcihowin is also the word for "living" and for "culture"; it's all the same word. It says something about our Nêhiyawak or Cree way of being in the world that our word for walking or journey can be the same word we use to talk about living. That's because acquiring the wisdom and knowledge needed for proper living is always a journey.[58]

I am fascinated by the linguistic intertwining of journeying, health, living, culture, and wisdom. That seems deeply coherent with the way that Jesus calls his apprentices to live. His call, as with any first-century rabbi, is "come, follow me." The invitation is to a journey of discovery, a full life immersion in the exploration and expression of heaven's kingdom in every aspect of our being. The framework for that is the two-part command to "love the Lord your God with all your heart, soul, mind, and strength" and "love your neighbor as yourself."[59] As we learn to love God, others, and ourselves well, the end result is growth in wisdom, which biblically speaking is the basis of a life well lived. It is the means by which we build a life that is sufficiently weird in the world as it is that when God gets the world God wants, we fit right in. Consider the parable of the wise and foolish builders, from the end of the Sermon on the Mount.[60] There, Jesus compares those who hear his instruction and follow it to one who builds a house on solid rock, strengthening it to withstand all of life's storms, as opposed to one who builds a house on sand and whose home is washed away when the rains come and the waters rise. Wisdom and action are combined to create an integrated life that is built on the foundation of Jesus's teachings, which span a wild range of instruction, most of which can only be embodied. There is no element of what Jesus says in the Sermon that suggests we can believe one thing and do another, or that our primary concern is for some other place and time, like after we die.

58. Aldred and Anderson, *Our Home on Treaty Land*, xiii.
59. Deut 6:5; Mark 12:30–31.
60. Matt 7:24–27.

This is not to suggest that resurrection and eternal life are inconsequential parts of Christian hope and belief, but that our salvation is a present and sensory experience—it is not only a heavenly concern; it's meant for here and now every bit as much as for there and then. To follow Jesus has to do with how we treat our friend and enemies, how we go about our work and worship, how we spend our money and our time, how we pray and how—and what—we produce.

If that is true, then the church that gathers in his name needs to be a community of training for that kind of integration. We must learn, together, to embody the hope that is ours. Our liturgies and practices, our meetings and budgets should be created and led with an eye towards shaping the gathered community in such a way that what happens on Sunday morning, or whenever the regular pattern of corporate worship brings us together, is not an isolated spiritual moment in an otherwise worldly-ordered life. I know of churches who have the phrase (or something like it) "Our worship begins now" painted over the door leading out of the church, as a visible reminder that nothing that has been said, sung, read, or prayed is meant to stay in some appropriately holy space. It is all meant to find shape in offices and on playgrounds; in classrooms and boardrooms and living rooms; in the checkout line at the grocery store, and on the bus to work, and in gatherings with friends and family. It is insufficient, disintegrated and disintegrating, and frankly uninteresting for us to proclaim the name of Jesus in our sanctuaries without living in his way in the world.

Incidentally, that is why it is so important to help one another develop practices of personal devotion, and to provide opportunities to connect with other Christians in other times and spaces. It is too much pressure on Sunday morning to make it do all the heavy lifting. We need regular practices that reorient us to who and how God is, if we will be intentional about living towards the world God wants. Without regular rhythms of prayer and Scripture reading, in particular—though there are countless spiritual practices that draw us towards God—we are subject temptations of other voices. That is most vividly demonstrated in the temptation stories, particularly Luke's version.[61]

The story begins before the Spirit leads (or chases, in Mark's version) Jesus into the wilderness, to fast and pray and be tempted by the devil. That scene has its roots in the story of Jesus's baptism.[62] There, Jesus rises out

---

61. Luke 4:1–13.
62. Luke 3:21–22.

INCARNATION

of the Jordan River, the heavens are torn open, and as the Spirit descends like a dove, we hear the divine voice: "You are my Son, the Beloved, with you I am well pleased." Later, in the wilderness, the devil comes to tempt Jesus, and the first sinister words are, "*If* you are the Son of God . . . ."[63] The temptations themselves are run-of-the-mill attempts to seduce Jesus with self-satisfaction, power, and spectacle. What is really at stake is if Jesus will listen to the voice of the One he calls Father, or some other voice. Will he trust who God says he is, or will he let the devil convince him to prove it?

Because evil is not creative, we can safely assume that most of the things that tempt us away from the ways and means of God are variations on the same theme. We are relentlessly exposed to calls to prove our worth, make a name for ourselves, clamor after power and authority—or at least buy things that make us look powerful and authoritative—temptations that seduce us towards arbitrary markers of success and value. Our temptations, whether we recognize them or not, are not the same as those leveled against Jesus, but neither are they much different. What is still at stake is whether or not we will trust what God says about us—that we are made in God's image, tirelessly loved by the One who is endlessly faithful, adopted into the heavenly family and availed of every privilege and glory given to Jesus as coheirs of heaven's kingdom with him—or will we settle for something else, something less? The way that we avoid settling for less than God wants for us, the way that we root and ground ourselves in God's love, that we are filled with all the fullness of God, is through regular attention to God, regular presence to the One who is eternally present to us. The primary way we do that is through prayer and Scripture, in private meditation and corporate worship.

Without regular immersion in God's word, consistent practices of prayer, and regular connection with others who are apprenticing under Jesus, it is nearly impossible to maintain the sort of faithfulness that Jesus invites us to. At best, we will end up with lives built on a mixed foundation, to return to our builders, and that cannot end in a sturdy home. We will always be worrying about the part built on sand, distracted from that which is built on solid rock, and at worst, we will simply fail to live the lives we are made for. We will miss the opportunity to truly incarnate the hope that saves the world.

All of this is, of course, much easier to say than to do. We are up against it in the journey towards integration and faithfulness, embodied

---

63. Luke 4:3.

wisdom in every word and deed. The call to follow Jesus in an incarnate apprenticeship, learning to love the things he loves and do the things that he does with all we are and have, is challenging work in a world where it is always easier to submit to the status quo. Our goal is *pimâcihowin*, to work daily for healthy, vibrant, flourishing communities that are prepared to embark on the long walk of growing in wisdom—or, as St. Paul puts it, growing up into the full stature of Christ.[64] And we have no other place to do that except in a world that often feels like it is languishing. We may not often find ourselves in places or moods perfectly conducive to our task. So, we depend on God's grace, without which faithfulness becomes an overwhelming requirement for the satisfaction of a demanding God. Perhaps an important part of being church together is helping each other recognize that while God's call may be demanding, we are also caught up in the joy of salvation, the joy of being counted among those who are "being saved."[65]

We cannot overstate the radical alternative to the way things are that Jesus calls us to. When St. John catches a vision of what God, in Christ, is up to, he can only call it a new heaven and a new earth.[66] And so, neither should we underestimate the extraordinary joy of joining in on God's redeeming work, of seeking the flourishing of others, of stewarding God's gifts and receiving the freedom for which the Son has set us free.[67] There are plenty of opportunities for soberness in church, and (as we will see) heartbreak is an appropriate and necessary part of faithfulness in a broken world. I contend that there should be many times more opportunities to rejoice in the Lord, to delight in each other, to wonder at creation, to find ourselves among the great cloud of witnesses and saints in every generation whose mouths are filled with laughter and whose tongues are full of singing at the goodness of God.[68] Scripture makes clear that there is virtually no situation in which that is impossible. It may be improbable; it can *feel* impossible. But the joy of the Lord is our strength, and we are caught up with the One whose determination is to wipe away every tear and turn our mourning to dancing. Part of an incarnate faith is allowing for that possibility wherever we are.

64. Eph 4:13.
65. Ps 51:12; Acts 2:47.
66. Rev 21:1.
67. John 8:36.
68. Ps 126.

Signpost 4

Discipline

Superficiality is the curse of our age. The doctrine of instant satisfaction is a primary spiritual problem. The desperate need today is not for a greater number of intelligent people, or gifted people, but for deep people.[1]

Come, O children, listen to me; I will teach you the fear of the LORD. Which of you desires life and covets many days to enjoy good? Keep your tongue from evil and your lips from speaking deceit. Depart from evil, and do good; seek peace, and pursue it.

PSALM 34:11–14

Discipline Is Weird

MY GUESS IS THAT no one is particularly surprised to find out that love and joy and peace are among what St. Paul calls "the Fruit of the Spirit."[2] Though we are an increasingly secular culture, we seem to still be okay with the notion of spirituality. When people tell me that they are "spiritual but not religious" the implication is generally that they believe things spiritual to fall under the category of general goodness, kindness, well-being, which

---

1. Foster, *Celebration of Discipline*, 1.
2. Gal 5:22–23.

is certainly true, in part.[3] But too often, "spiritual" tends to remain ethereal, vague, ineffable. To be "spiritual," in the way that our culture allows for such a thing, tends to mean allowing that there is something beyond the end of our noses—some greater purpose, energy, some animating force we cannot quite define. But that force may or may not have anything to do with our actual lives. It may have something to do with the way we respond to the beauty of creation, or a willingness to "live and let live," or comfort with the fact that not everything in life is perfectly understandable or controllable. But when the spiritual contradicts our basic desires or threatens our personal sovereignty, it is easily set aside or forgot altogether. After all, "spiritual" is just, sort of, *out there*. It is not at play in our day jobs, or entertainment, the way we spend our money or use our bodies.

The Bible, not to mention Jesus, is not particularly interested in that kind of spirituality. When St. Paul sets out the feast of the Fruit of the Spirit, the list culminates in "self-control." Self-control is a gift that can only be exercised in the particularities of everyday life. Self-control requires keeping a rein not only on our thoughts and desires, but with the very ways that we are in the world, whatever the circumstances. And that requires discipline. Discipline, in a culture that prizes self-expression and personal fulfillment over just about anything else, is weird.

Discipline is weird precisely because it requires self-limitation, choosing to do some things and not others. It is about depth, not just breadth. It requires intentionality, persistence, "a long obedience in the same direction."[4] It requires eschewing instant gratification in favor of long-term gain. Of course, we have plenty of examples of discipline outside of the church. Most religions have an inherent call to discipline of one form or another. Social media is full of health and fitness influencers challenging us to focus on one physical goal or another. Financial advisors will tell us that our long-term financial stability is built on the responsible use and saving of our money in the short-term, avoiding the temptations of every present desire for a future benefit. There are countless self-help books and podcasts whose primary intention is to train us in a disciplined way of being. I have recently been receiving ads on social media for a "self-care pet."

---

3. In my experience, "spiritual but not religious" tends to imply a commitment to an inherent goodness within oneself, if not the world. "Spiritual" is assumed to be coequal with what we believe to be right and good. The problem is that when we deny the possibility of spiritual evil, we lose the capacity to talk coherently about a lot of the destructive realities that are experienced in this world.

4. Peterson, *Long Obedience*.

DISCIPLINE

This is a smartphone app that rewards good and healthy decision-making by coordinating self-care practices with the "care" of a digital "pet." Floss your teeth, or do some push-ups, or complete your to-do list, practice a few minutes of mindfulness, and "Finch" is taken care of.[5] We seem to recognize the personal benefits of discipline, but have a hard time sorting out how to embrace it.

Perhaps what makes Christian discipline, self-control in the Jesus Way, weirdest is that whatever benefits are derived from it may or may not be accrued to us personally. Followers of Jesus have a habit of doing things that are not obviously self-improving or beneficial. We are learning to "have the same mind as Christ," whose impulse is radical self-giving for the sake of love.[6] Consider the discipline of giving tithes or offerings, a willful act of generosity that may not even benefit those in our immediate sphere of influence. To give as an act of worship is to surrender our gifts to whatever God chooses to do with them. There may be attendant advantages, but they are inherently secondary. Science tells us that generosity is good for us, and that, I believe, is by design. But to purposefully choose downward mobility, offering up resources that could be used for our own pleasure or security, is weird when we are so often told that any limit on our personal happiness is an affront to our dignity.

We have already considered that prayer is weird in and of itself, but lots of religious instruction and secular wisdom testifies to the personal benefit of prayer and meditation. A scientific study of Tibetan Buddhist monks has demonstrated that a disciplined practice of meditation has significant positive effects on personal well-being and our capacity to self-regulate in the face of stresses and traumas.[7] All sorts of secular health influencers attest to the many benefits of even short practices of mindfulness in reducing anxiety and stress, improving attention and overall health. But when Christians pray, our goal is not so much self-mastery or self-emptying, or even inner peace, beneficial as those things clearly are. Our goal is surrender to Someone outside ourselves.[8] The goal of Christian prayer is submission to

---

5. From the iPhone app store: "Meet your new self-care best friend! Finch is a self-care pet app that helps you feel prepared and positive, one day at a time. Take care of yourself! Choose from a wide variety of self-care exercises that are personalized for you."

6. Phil 2:5–11.

7. See the documentary film *Mission: Joy—Finding Happiness in Troubled Times*, featuring His Holiness the Dalai Lama and Archbishop Desmond Tutu and directed by Louie Psihoyos.

8. There are certainly Christian prayer practices, such as Centering Prayer, or the disciplines of silence and solitude, that are similar and offer similar benefits to other

both the will of God, *and* to becoming the person God made each of us to be. Prayer is our primary means of participating in God's redemptive work in the world; it is the discipline of conforming our will to God's, trusting that God's will for us is very good. It is the means by which we live into our ultimate desire—and desperate need—for God's commonwealth to come on earth as in heaven.

At the heart of our Song for the Strange, the pray-er invites us to come as children and learn what life with this God is like. He calls us to particular and intentional practices of disciplining our tongues, doing good, seeking peace, turning from evil. He does offer this instruction as the key to a good life, but within the arc of Scripture, that is a secondary benefit. The primary benefit of discipline is finding our proper place with and in God, for the world—that is what constitutes fullness of life in the Way of Jesus. We cannot separate the pursuit of a good life from the call to bless, boast in, and magnify the Lord, with which the psalm begins. We cannot separate the pursuit of a good life from the Fear-of-the-Lord—fear which is not scared or timid, but awe-filled: the staggering awareness that in God's presence we are with the One whose ways and thoughts are far above ours, whose power and purpose outstrip our best efforts, and whose love, faithfulness, and grace are extravagantly more than we can ask or imagine.[9]

For those of us in the modern, Western world, Christian discipline is a determined pursuit of God and the things God loves, over and against the myriad ways we are wooed to pursue our own self-interest and self-improvement. This pursuit requires the development of practices that keep us facing God, contending and communing with God—practices that keep us looking to the Lord so that we might reflect the radiance for which we are made. These practices may be daily or weekly or monthly actions, or they may be appropriate for a season.

One of the undervalued seasons of formation in many Protestant traditions is Lent, the forty-day season (not counting Sundays, which are always a celebration of Jesus's resurrection) that leads up to Holy Week. Lent begins with the supremely countercultural marking of Ash Wednesday, when we get together and remind each other that we are going to die: "Remember that you are dust, and to dust you shall return." Then many people take on a practice that directs their attention to God, such as generosity to the poor, or they abstain from something that embodies a spirit of

---

traditions and practices. But I would contend that the goal is different.

9. Peterson, *Practice Resurrection*, 235.

sacrificial worship, echoing Jesus's forty-day preparation in the wilderness for his ministry.[10] I have a colleague who once wore the same nondescript dress every day throughout Lent, as a way of paying attention to the ways in which vanity and self-expression distracted her from love of God and neighbor, and as a way of resisting a culture of unbridled accumulation and relentless self-concern. In the church, female leaders are often subject to scrutiny about their clothing in ways that men are not. So, this practice also pushed against the misogyny and patriarchy that continue to plague our culture, including in the church. It was weird, but effective, both personally and for her congregation. When the season was over, she returned to a more diverse wardrobe. But both she and her community were more deeply aware of the ways in which our tireless concern for the ways that we present ourselves in the world can hinder our awareness of, and participation in, what God wants to do in and through us.

Discipline Is Political

Discipline is political because as we undertake individual practices of attention and submission to God and what God loves, we and our communities are invariably formed in ways that look more and more like Jesus. Christian disciplines regularly put us in positions of active resistance to the things in the world, and in our particular cultures, that are dehumanizing and destructive. David calls those of us who "desire life" and "covet many days to enjoy good" to join him in what are often countercultural practices. As people learning the Fear-of-the-Lord, life and goodness must be more than is on offer in so much advertising. It must be more than a comfortable retirement, or the latest toys, or the most fashionable things that rust and rot and fade away. Desiring life and enjoying good in biblical terms is choosing formation in the ways and means of the God who made this world teem with life and called it good, and very good, sometimes over and against the self-indulgence that is regularly encouraged by the world around us.

Even more, discipline is political because it assumes an end goal that includes us but is beyond us. It is nothing short of a willingness to live towards the world as God wants it. It assumes that the world is being guided in a particular direction, an end coherent with the creative desire of God. The fancy Greek word for that is *telos*. The word contains within it the assumption that the world and everything in it is heading somewhere, that

---

10. Luke 4:1–13.

there is an ultimate goal. We are not caught in an endless spiral, but all of history is moving towards the day when all things will be made new, when every tear will be wiped away and every belly filled, when we will splash in the River of Life that flows from heaven's throne and rest ourselves beneath the Tree of Life, whose leaves are for the healing of the nations.[11]

But what does it look like to live that now? What does it mean to have that future pulling us towards itself? The mixed blessing of discipleship to Jesus is that he takes us seriously as individuals. This is not an invitation to individualism, but the delightful fact that he refuses to love generally and chooses to take our lives with cosmic and particular seriousness. In the Gospels, whenever Jesus heals a person it's never in quite the same way. Sometimes he touches them, sometimes they touch him. Sometimes he gives the word and they are healed, sometimes the healing involves spit and mud. Sometimes it's instantaneous, and sometimes it takes a couple tries. Sometimes demons are cast out, and sometimes withered limbs are restored to full strength. This should probably incline us to understand that the way that Jesus will heal each of us of our disordered loves and mangled motives, how he will satisfy our "hard hungers"[12] and renew life where it is withered in us, will be different. This is a mixed blessing because it means that blanket cures and black-and-white, one-size-fits-all answers are not going to cut it, unfortunately. It would be easier if it were otherwise. But not nearly so life-giving.

Of course, there are disciplines well-attested by saints in every generation that can help us grow in and maintain our commitment to the will and way of God in the world. Richard Foster's seminal work, *Celebration of Discipline: The Path to Spiritual Growth* is an introduction to many of these. As we pay attention to the life and ministry of Jesus, it is clear that there are practices such as prayer, fasting, service, and solitude that will be a part of any maturing apprenticeship to his way. But there are any number of ways that we can grow in love of God and neighbor. In fact, anything that directs our attention to God, in gratitude or hope or wonder, can be a discipline for Christian living. Regular exercise is a means by which we care for the gift that is our bodies. A glass of wine with loved ones can awaken thankfulness for the gifts of the earth and the joys of companionship. Creating art can bring our hearts in tune with the One who creates out of love and pure delight. Hiking can teach us to treasure the non-human creation with which

---

11. Rev 22:1–2.
12. Job 30:3.

we are so inextricably entwined, but so often fail to notice. Cooking a meal for others draws us into the web of relations on which we are dependent for food and flourishing.

Even what Kathleen Norris calls the "quotidian mysteries," the daily—sometimes drudging—tasks that sustain a household, laundry and dishwashing and sweeping the floor, can become ways to be more attentive to the Holy Spirit's movement in our lives and relationships. She writes:

> We want life to have meaning, we want fulfillment, healing and even ecstacy, but the human paradox is that we find these things by starting where we are, not where we wish we were. We must look for blessings to come from unlikely, everyday places—out of Galilee, as it were—and not in spectacular events, such as the coming of a comet.[13]

My wife is a vocational homemaker. She currently has employment that takes her out of the house most days, but some of her deepest joys, the things that make her feel like she is doing what she is called to do, consist in creating and maintaining a space for our family to thrive and for others to be welcomed into.[14] She has been inspired by the avant-garde artist Mierle Ukeles and her Maintenance Art Manifesto—an invitation to take seriously the care of people, things, and spaces as an artistic endeavor. Although Ukeles does not publicly attribute any particular faith commitment to her work, she is the daughter of a rabbi, and it is hard not to see the influence of that fact. Her work as the artist in residence for the New York City Sanitation Department participates in the Edenic call to steward and care for creation and to do the daily work that sustains the conditions for communal flourishing. Often, it is work that not only sustains, but restores, heals, and dignifies what is otherwise disregarded and disdained.

All this demonstrates that spiritual disciplines, the containers for self-control, cannot be reduced to handy lists of thou-shalts and thou-shalt-nots. Discipline in the Way of Jesus requires attentiveness, discernment, openness, and obedience to the Spirit's movements. Often, rather than straightforward instruction, a fruitful image is more helpful for developing a life of joyful discipline. Jesus frequently makes use of plant imagery when teaching about what a kingdom of God oriented life looks like. Parables

---

13. Norris, *Quotidian Mysteries*, 10.

14. Frederick Buechner's oft quoted aphorism stands the test of time. He says that one's vocation is "the place where your deep gladness and the world's deep hunger meet." Buechner, *Beyond Words*, 405.

of mustard seeds and even fruitless fig trees can be helpful images for measuring our spiritual health. While those were surely chosen for their familiarity, it is instructive that he did not resort to mechanical or militaristic imagery—which were surely available to him—as we so often seem to. There is something about discipline in the Way of Jesus that is at once contained and limited, but also full of fruitful and surprising possibility.

My favorite biblical image of the joy and fruitfulness of discipline is Psalm 1:

> 1 Happy are those
> who do not follow the advice of the wicked
> or take the path that sinners tread
> or sit in the seat of scoffers,
> 2 but their delight is in the law of the Lord,
> and on his law they meditate day and night.
> 3 They are like trees
> planted by streams of water,
> which yield their fruit in its season,
> and their leaves do not wither.
> In all that they do, they prosper.
> 4 The wicked are not so
> but are like chaff that the wind drives away.
> 5 Therefore the wicked will not stand in the judgment
> nor sinners in the congregation of the righteous,
> 6 for the Lord watches over the way of the righteous,
> but the way of the wicked will perish.

This entry into the psalter, the gate that shapes the rest of our primary prayerbook, begins with the discipline of discernment and commitment to an intentional pursuit of righteousness—right relationship with God, our truest selves, each other, and creation. As we live towards the world God wants, we are careful about who dictates the terms of our lives; we resist the advice of the wicked—life hacks that prize efficiency and impersonality and selfishness. We guard the uses of our energies, refusing to spend time moving along paths that take us away from God and the things God loves. We protect our minds from cynicism and disdain, and our mouths from language that tears down rather than builds up. We develop the discipline of delighting in the law of the Lord, the ways and means of God in our lives and in the world. We let the things of God, every spiritual fruit, root in us so that our attention is continually guided by the breath of God. To meditate on the law of the Lord is not to simply memorize Bible verses, but to chew on, gnaw at, suck all the nutrients out of the Scriptures and traditions that shape us and strengthen us for the work of heaven's kingdom.

And when we do that, the psalmist says, we are like trees, planted by streams of water, bearing our proper fruit—exercising our vocations—and participating in God's ecosystem as it is established wherever we are. That image alone should trigger a vibrant imagination for what it means to be living faithfully, living as we are made to live. What sorts of things plant us by the river of life? How are we made to contribute to the living world around us? I have a friend who is a bit of a gardening nut. She regularly courts the ire of the by-law officer, planting all manner of vegetables in places that her county says should only have grass. One of her deepest commitments as she cultivates the plot of land she lives on is the practice of permaculture, which takes for granted the interconnectedness of ecosystems, and therefore such gardens are established and nurtured in ways that mimic natural, sustainable, and resilient systems. It integrates rather than segregates crops. Plants and trees and groundcover that are mutually supporting and beneficial are planted in proximity to each other or even layered for maximum contact. It's a way of growing food that reduces waste, that observes and tends to the interactions of earth, plants, animals, pollinators, and the humans who will work and benefit from the garden's fruitfulness.

As we consider the tree we will be, fruitful and lush, we ought not imagine that somehow the tree is solitary. Its roots are woven into the earth, its branches home to creatures furred and feathered, its leaves provide safety and shade, its fruit nourishes. It releases oxygen as it breathes in carbon dioxide. It stretches up towards the sun, and its roots prevent soil erosion. This should tell us that a life of discipline is not a life of self-containment, of cutting ourselves off from the world, or rigid asceticism. It is all about how we are *in* the world, how we play our part in the garden God is planting, interacting with the life all around us for the sake of mutual flourishing. When David calls us near to learn the things that lead to life, they are invariably relational things. How we speak, what it means to resist evil—the spiritual inclinations and systemic structures that inhibit life and liveliness—doing good and seeking peace, all of these things must be considered and enacted communally. It is easy enough to watch what we say, when we do not have to worry about the words and actions of others. Resisting systemic evil gets a whole lot easier if we cloister ourselves off from the world. If we only had to do good and seek peace by ourselves, this

Christian life would be a snap. But it is not good for us to be alone.[15] Left to our own devices, we can never experience the fullness of life for which we are made—even if there are days when we might like to give it a shot. Once more, discipline is not just about us and our little lives; it has everything to do with how we are present to God, for the world; it shapes us as humans in community; it is political.

Discipline Is Presence

What is clear as we watch Jesus is that the disciplines that shape his life and ministry are not about getting away from the world, but they move him deeper and deeper into it. They do not save him from the cross; they launch him towards it. They are not about developing sacred practices that elevate him above others, but about learning to love, heal, speak, and serve as the Father loves, heals, speaks, and serves. Discipline in the Way of Jesus is primarily an act of attentive, loving presence to God and neighbor. This means that discipline in the Way of Jesus is not simply about trying harder—though, as Dallas Willard says, grace is opposed to earning, not effort—but primarily discipline is the humble reception of the goodness of God and the willful sharing of that goodness with all we are and have.

Every spiritual discipline, every act of faithful self-control that deepens our participation in God's redemption story, is an exercise in getting beyond ourselves, resisting the world's encouragement to double-down on self-interest, self-protection, self-obsession. Disciplines make us aware that we are interconnected and interdependent. It is no wonder that our smartphones, the devices that make self-centeredness so easy and convenient, are also among the greatest hindrances to our formation in Christ. Although humans have always been eager for distraction and resistant to boredom, the current availability of just about anything in the world in the palm of our hands is a unique burden for those who want to be about what God is about. The sheer ubiquity of little screens, serving up any number of diversions and opportunities to self-satisfy, radically hinders our capacity to be present in the world. Many of us are rarely where our bodies are, which means we are rarely actively participating in what God is up to, in us, others, or the wider world. Which means, in turn, we rarely open ourselves up to fully receiving all that God wants for us, let alone sharing it with others. It is hard to believe that God can and will do more in us and through us

15. Gen 2:18.

than we can ask or imagine, when everything we could want, every whim of imagination is only a few keystrokes away.

Of course, it is a lie that everything we could want or imagine is available to us. We are inevitably limited. And the staggering numbers of people afflicted by anxiety and depression, fear and hopelessness, suggest that we are still deeply hungry for more than we can come up with on our own. Discipline invites us into a space where that hunger can be satisfied. Jesus says, "blessed are you who hunger and thirst for righteousness, for you will be filled."[16] St. Paul prays that we would "know the love of Christ that surpasses knowledge, so that you may be filled with all the fullness of God."[17] We are made for more than our own best efforts, or even our wildest imaginations. Spiritual disciplines—the classic ones, or the ones that feed our specific, God-beloved souls—are the acts of presence that make space for us to receive the soul-satisfaction we long for.

It is not only endless hours of screen time that hinder our availability to God and others or infringe on time that could be spent more fruitfully. Our world is frenetic and noisy in ways unimaginable to previous generations. The sociologist Hartmut Rosa says life today is like running up the down escalator—we have to work harder and harder simply to stay in the same place.[18] It is exhausting for lots of folks just to make it through the day. There is always more to do. There is always another demand on our time. Carving out space for spiritual disciplines can feel like another task to add to our already bloated schedules. Part of what makes discipline an act of self-control is that it invariably means not adding things to our busy lives but removing things so that we can live at a saner pace. I heard someone remark once that if we are too busy for prayer and Scripture, we are busier than God made us to be. If we are too busy to seek God's presence, and to tend to the people around us, then we might well be successful by worldly standards, but we are failing at the life we are made for.

Often, when I imagine myself to be too busy to pray, or that the day's demands require me to buzz through a quiet time in the morning so that I can get on to the important stuff, I think of Susanna Wesley. Although in the church we tend to be most familiar with her two famous sons, John and Charles, Susanna was mother to eleven children, for whose education she

---

16. Matt 5:6.

17. Eph 3:19.

18. I heard him say this in the 2024 G. Peter Kaye lecture, given at the Vancouver School of Theology, March 1, 2024.

took primary and intense responsibility. Her husband was a problematic character, who bankrupted his family and occasionally abandoned them for long stretches, pursuing his own passions and interests (none of which made a lasting impression on the world). Her house burnt down twice. I have a hard time imagining how I would manage the extraordinary demands on this extraordinary woman. And yet, in the midst of it all, she managed to raise her kids, keep her house, create several works of theological depth, and inspire two of modern Christianity's most important voices. The lasting image of Susanna, in my mind, is of her prayer practice. She was well known to throw her apron over her head, at which point her children knew that mom was praying and not to be disturbed. That was her ersatz prayer room. Where she could not go off into the wilderness, or shut a door for privacy, she made a space that allowed her time and space to commune with God, praying and listening, attuning herself to the movements of the Holy Spirit. And from there, everything else flowed—her resilience, her family and home life, her writing and teaching. No doubt she understood that there was entirely too much to be done to rush her time with God. She prioritized the discipline of prayer and let her life be shaped by that, not the other way around.

One of the challenges of discipline is that, for many of us, it conjures up images of folks not much into fun, people of little joy—the rigidly ascetic or tiresomely stoic. Perhaps we imagine a life defined by restriction, or neurotic calorie counting. Maybe think of something imposed on us, even if performed by us, a consequence of our failure to measure up to a standard set by someone else. But that is not a biblical imagination about what discipline means. It certainly does not stack up against Ps 1, or the urgent joy of Ps 34. Biblically, there is a consistent connection between discipline and desire—the longing of a lover for their beloved. It both stems from desire and nurtures desire. On the bulletin board over my desk, I have a cue card on which I have scribbled, *Give me the desire to seek you more and more; and when that desire fails, give me the discipline to do so.* This is the basic commitment of biblical faith and Christian discipleship. To meditate on the law of God, to seek the face of Jesus is a response to the deepest desires of our hearts, to know and be known as deeply as possible. It is an act of love and devotion to the One who loves us more than we know, who has pursued us in goodness and mercy, and who invites us to live in and from that reality. The disciplined pursuit of God, the faithful determination to orient our lives towards heaven's kingdom in all we do, cannot result in moroseness. As Karl Barth says, "The theologian who labors without joy is not a theologian at all."[19] And anyone committed to the Way of Jesus is necessarily a theologian, one determined to know God as fully as we are able to on this side of things.

Discipline Is a Way of Life

It is probably insufficient to say that Christian discipline is a way of life. It is not merely a way; it is the means of life. It is the way that what Scripture calls "life that is truly life" and "life abundant" takes root. It is the way that we become that tree, planted by streams of water. It is the way that we learn to control our tongues, resist evil, do good, pursue peace, in the way that Jesus does. It is our apprenticeship in his way, the way that we are formed by the kingdom of God, not the kingdoms of the world.

I think it is indicative of a deep hunger for a coherent, integrated life within the church that there is a growing number of influential voices—particularly in certain Evangelical traditions—and whole communities of faith advocating for the practice of developing an intentional Rule of Life.[20] Those who do so are clear that all of us have a Rule of Life; the question is whether it is intentional or simply imposed upon us by the demands and vicissitudes of the world. We all have rhythms and practices that shape us, forming us in particular ways and towards particular ends. None of us can avoid the influence of others, of the systems we find ourselves in, of the cultural demands and expectations that are sometimes explicit but are often subtle suggestions whispered in our ears, tempting us onto a path other than Jesus's. We are tempted by all manner of things that mangle the image of God we are made in and distract us from the *telos* we are made for.

Tyler Staton, lead pastor of Bridgetown Church in Portland, Oregon, and director of 24-7 Prayer USA, uses the image of an anchor to explain the value of a Rule of Life. He notes that when you are on a boat that is anchored, you do not notice the anchor until the boat drifts a little too far. Then there is a tug back to the center. Another image is of a trellis, that creates a structure for climbing plants to thrive. Many plants that climb—like grapes, for instance—will survive if they are not supported by a trellis. They

---

19. Morrison, "Happy 130th Birthday."

20. I am always inspired by Tyler Staton on the topic of a Rule of Life. This talk at an event in Vancouver has been fruitful for my own thinking (Staton, "Reviving the Ancient Practice of a Rule of Life").

may even produce big leaves, but they will not produce fruit like they are made to. A Rule of Life is not a stringent list of rules and regulations, but a guide to fruitfulness, an anchor that keeps us where we are meant to be. "Rule" comes from the Latin *regula*, a straight stick that points us in the right direction.

A Rule of Life, intentional or implicit, is effectively a docket of disciplines, a way to keep ourselves oriented in a particular direction. For those of us who would follow Jesus, a Rule ought to craft our lives in such a way that the ways that we spend our time, our money, our work life, the way we establish our priorities, the media we consume keeps us walking in step with the Spirit.[21] Again, whether we choose it or not, something is going to pull and prod in these areas of our lives. As much as our culture prizes individualism and self-expression, we are invariably shaped by the people and places that surround us, even if those are only coming at us through screens. If we are not diligent in our attention to God, aware of the ways that we get disintegrated in our discipleship—living as though parts of our life are open to God and others off-limits—we find ourselves living in dissonance and distraction, when what we are made for is beauty and life wide open to what the Maker of heaven and earth has in store.

There is always a danger that discipline, self-control, a Rule of Life, however we want to think about the call to Christian faithfulness, can end up becoming an exercise in "works righteousness." We can begin to imagine that if we just do all the right things, we will invariably get the life we want. That is the promise of so many social media gurus and life-coaches: we can work our way into some version of righteousness—whether defined by the Bible or the culture we inhabit. And while many of us manage to cobble together a fairly satisfying life, the promise of self-fulfillment or even earning our standing in God's presence always comes up empty. Worse, when things go sideways (and they will, at some point) we may be convinced that it is due to a failure of faithfulness, or that we simply did not try hard enough, that we are being punished for one shortcoming or another. The fear of that failure to measure up is at the root of so much anxiety and trauma in contemporary Western culture. A spiritual discipline that exacerbates that is no spiritual discipline at all. Even someone as intensely disciplined as St. Paul or St. James recognizes that their diligence in practice and prayer, their unfettered commitment to following Jesus wherever he leads, always leads them even further into the heart of love. This is why Paul can encourage

---

21. Gal 5:25.

his Philippian congregation to "Rejoice in the Lord always!" even while sitting in a prison cell.[22] Our spiritual disciplines can draw us to the throne of mercy with boldness and wonder, whatever else is going on. Practicing those disciplines, daily exercising the Spirit's gift of self-control, will mean that we have access to the grace and mercy and peace beyond understanding or circumstance, wherever we find ourselves.

That is the goal of discipline, the aim of self-control: to keep our eyes firmly fixed on the One who made us and loves us, who has crossed heaven and earth to be with us and for us, and from whom nothing in heaven, earth, or hell will separate us. When we are moving towards that reality, we are becoming like that tree, planted by streams of water, receiving the nourishment we need and participating in the world the way we are made to, playing our role in God's ecosystem. As much as I love the familiar words of Ps 1, I appreciate Nan C. Merrill's rendering and reimagining of the ancient words:

> Blessed are those
>   who walk hand in hand
>   with goodness,
>   who stand beside virtue,
>   who sit in the seat of truth;
> For their delight is in the Spirit of Love,
>   and in Love's heart they dwell
> day and night.
> They are like trees planted by
>   streams of water,
>   that yield fruit in due season,
>   and their leaves flourish;
> And in all they do, they give life.[23]

"In all they do, they give life" is a good summary of what it means to be growing in the Way of Jesus, the goal of discipline. If I were to advocate for one discipline that we need to grow in, beside prayer and Scripture reading, which are basic necessities for maturing Christians, it would be Sabbath keeping. I want to begin this advocacy by acknowledging that in some contexts the capacity to stop for a day is a privilege. The single parent who must work multiple jobs, the person caught in economic systems whose chief aim is to make money for the already rich while paying labor

---

22. Phil 4:4.
23. Merrill, *Psalms*, 1.

just enough to keep them bound and dependent, young families who only see each other one day a week, all may find a twenty-four-hour Sabbath a significant burden, if not impossibility. As with any spiritual discipline, we cannot guilt people into practicing it; we cannot bully people into life. However, in most cases, the seeming impossibility of Sabbath has more to do with unhealthy rhythms and our profound formation by a culture that insists that if we are not producing, then we are not valuable. Or, if our kids are not manically scheduled, they will fall behind, or miss out, or they won't grow into well-rounded adults. Truth be told, clergy are often the worst at this. Many of us are, as Stanley Hauerwas so characteristically puts it, "quivering masses of availability."[24] The urge to respond whenever called, and—worse—to look worth our paycheck, to keep the church running when it feels like no one else will, to be of value to our community, these are serious hazards of pastoral work. Not, of course, that we should refuse to respond in the case of emergency, or abdicate pastoral responsibility, and we do have an important role in the life and work of the church. We are often the only ones being paid to show up. But we face a significant spiritual danger when our value is tied up in being needed. It can look a lot like pastoral care and concern, but a closer look might suggest that it has more to do with ego than holiness, more to do with the expectations of capitalism than faithfulness to the Way of Jesus.

It is a radical witness to stop for a day, to work six days and then rest. The Bible cites two reasons to do this. The first is that God did it, as we read in the creation poem in Gen 1. The second is that we are not slaves: Sabbath is the defining act of God's people when they are brought out of slavery in Egypt; this is how they will learn to live in freedom. Only slaves work every day. Free people rest. I am convinced that this second reason is every bit as important for us in the twenty-first century as it was when the Israelites took their first steps from under the shadow of Egypt. Because unless we can receive our own freedom, delight in our own humanity—not as units of production but living, breathing, fully alive, and God-bearing people—we will not work for the freedom of others, we will not fully delight in the humanity of others. Only in allowing ourselves to receive the grace and goodness of God when we are accomplishing nothing will we be bearers of that grace and goodness when we are undertaking the things that fill our workdays. If we want to be people who give life in all we do, we have to grow in awareness of what a holy rhythm of life looks like.

24. Dash, "Quivering Mass of Availability."

While a full-day Sabbath may not be (or seem) possible, I am a big proponent of "micro-Sabbaths." Smaller pauses. Maybe half a day. Maybe starting with a single hour where we do one thing that pampers our soul.[25] For some, that will be a creative pursuit. My wife spends her lunch break knitting or darning, rather than getting through a few more emails. For others, reading a novel or poetry will be an oasis. Some may just want to sit on a park bench, or take a walk, or take a nap. The point is simply to stop being "productive" in any sense that the world would recognize, to feel and know our freedom in Christ, and to reclaim our humanity when it is reduced to what we do.

What would it look like to take responsibility for the care of one another as a community committed to rhythms that draw us deeper into the life of God, especially for those for whom Sabbath pauses are made challenging by a particular season or circumstance of life? Could we babysit for parents of young kids, so that they can go on a date? Could we prepare a nice meal for the single person consumed by work and too tired to cook when they get home? Could we volunteer to do tasks for others, so that when there is a break in the action they do not have to default to getting all the "other stuff" of life done? Could we get really radical and start to organize our community finances so that those trapped in precarious financial positions that keep them working multiple jobs can quit one? Every bit as important as helping others—and for some of us, as radical—would we let ourselves be helped into saner rhythms? This really is about our collective humanity, not only our individual leisure. By pausing regularly, we can work in holy rhythms to our frantic worlds, reorienting ourselves to the One who says, "Come to me, all you who are weary and carrying heavy burdens, and I will give you rest. Take my yoke upon you and learn from me, for I am gentle and humble in heart, and you will find rest for your souls. For my yoke is easy, and my burden is light."[26]

---

25. I got this phrase from John Mark Comer, in the "Sabbath Practice" video series.
26. Matt 11:28–30.

Signpost 5

Lament

I am beginning to despair
and can see only two choices:
either go crazy or turn holy.[1]

The Lord is close to the brokenhearted, and saves the crushed in spirit.

PSALM 34:18

Lament Is Weird

THE POET ADÉLIA PRADO confronts us with an improbable, and I think, breathtaking choice: go crazy or turn holy in the face of despair. It is improbable, because it feels as though there must be something in between. How about we start by turning off the news for a bit? Surely, there are any number of options to scroll through before we hit either insanity or holiness. But I find it breathtaking because it feels so true. There does not seem to be a bottom to the pit of pain and brokenness in the world. And facing that, if we are able, means coming face to face with a near absolute futility, our human frailty. It is hard to imagine what any one of us can possibly do. The challenges are vertiginous. It is crazy-making.

---

1. Prado, "Serenade," 60.

And yet. It is also in that space of despondency and despair when we might find ourselves most available to receive this astonishing promise: "The Lord is close to the brokenhearted."

The world as most of us experience it does not do lament very well. We have gotten good at outrage, sadness, hopelessness. We know all about disenfranchisement and cynicism. But lament is another thing altogether. In cultural contexts that tend to push us to the extremes of insufferable happiness or self-righteous anger, lament is weird.[2] Lament is weird because it has less to do with our personal feelings than it does with our conviction that God cares about those feelings. Lament is the act of bringing all that stuff that threatens to overwhelm us, from the personal crises and traumas that punctuate our lives, to the devastation that so often plagues the world, into the presence of God. Lament is the outpouring of a holy brokenheartedness. It can be the psalmist crying out, "How long, O Lord?"[3] It can contain the anger that yearns for enemies to feel the fullness of divine wrath, to feel something like the pain they have caused.[4] It holds our frustration at the state of things in our lives and in the world, like Isaiah insisting that "we sinned because *you* turned away," demanding that God remember just who is God in this situation.[5] Lament is the words we find at the end of our ropes, even when we have no confidence that things will get better; it is what we feel and sound like, what we dare to pray, in the company of the one who voices the devastating prayer we call Ps 88.

2. The difference between happiness and joy is well attested. However, recognizing that difference makes clear why happiness can so often look and feel insufferable. Happiness is etymologically related to "happenings" or "happens." It is contingent upon the relative pleasantness of our current circumstances. Happiness is therefore not, in and of itself, a bad thing. Sometimes our circumstances are supremely pleasant. But the felt requirement to present as happy to those around us, or who follow us on social media, so often requires ignoring swaths of life that are much less so. Joy, on the other hand, is not contingent on what is currently happening, but on what has happened in the past, a completed reality, and a solid hope for the future based on that personal knowledge or communal witness. For Christians, happiness may be a present reality, but our joy is rooted in God's tireless faithfulness and the fact that we have caught a glimpse of heaven's coming kingdom in the life, death, resurrection, and ascension of Jesus. Our joy is rooted in the fact that there is nothing in heaven, earth, or hell that can separate us from the love of God, in Christ Jesus our Lord (Rom 8:31–39). And so, like Paul and Silas singing in prison, aching from another round of corporal punishment, our joy can find its way into any circumstance—even the depths of lament.

3. Ps 13:1.

4. For instance, Pss 3 or 127.

5. Isa 64:5.

That is what separates lament from other expressions of emotion, even ones that look and sound awfully similar: in the end, lament is prayer. It is the bold determination to bring *everything*, even the stuff that feels totally inappropriate in church—violence and unforgiveness and vengeance and despondency, things not meant for polite company—into the throne room of heaven. It's to drop the worst and weakest of ourselves and the world at God's feet, in the audacious conviction that God will receive it and do something about it. It's to cast our cares upon the Lord, *because he cares for us*.[6] Even Ps 88—which, unlike most psalms of lament, never makes a turn towards hopefulness; it just ends in bitterness and pain—is still a prayer, perfectly and painfully appropriate for those who take God seriously. When Jesus cries out from the cross, "My God, my God, why have you forsaken me?" it is even still a prayer to the One who is, now and ever, "*my God.*"[7] Those who know how to lament know that it is okay not to be okay in the presence of God.

What might be weirdest about lament is not simply the willingness to voice feelings that are often only articulated in private, or repressed altogether, but the fact that it is ultimately evidence that we are fully alive in this world. It is to take the fullness of our humanity as seriously as God does. It is to live with eyes wide open, refusing to turn away from the pain that is so regularly splashed across news feeds or lying on the street corner, embracing a deep awareness that the world is not as it was made to be. Lament is an act of resistance to the narcotics of consumerism and fleeting happiness and self-concern, instead pursuing the promise that the Lord is close to the brokenhearted. Lament trusts that God is not pleased with the mess of things either, and that God is determined to redeem, restore, and heal us and everything else—even on days when that hope seems out of reach. Lament opens us up to the fact that the opposite of joy is not sadness, or pain, or anger. The opposite of joy is numbness, the inability or unwillingness to experience the fullness of life, both in green pastures and death's valley.[8] For those of us who can easily spend our days absorbing whatever a given algorithm feeds us, based on a limited range of emotion or interest that a machine determines will suit us—whether pornographic or propagandist,

---

6. 1 Pet 5:7.
7. Matt 27:46, quoting Ps 22:1.
8. Wirzba, *Love's Braided Dance*, 21; Ps 23.

it matters very little—a willingness to open ourselves to the fullness of human experience is a rebellious and faithful, even holy, act.⁹

It seems reasonable to assume that this is why so many of the psalms contain lament, often right alongside soaring joy. Or why books like Job and Lamentations made the canonical cut. Our ancestors in faith and prayer understood that we cannot be truly faithful to God, who has given all of Godself in wondrous and even vulnerable ways, if we are not willing to give all of ourselves in return. To lament, especially when it contains anger, is an act of trust that God is not deterred from divine pursuit of us when we are not well, spiritually, physically, or emotionally. It is okay not to be okay in the presence of God, as it is in any truly intimate relationship, only infinitely more so. It may feel weird, and even inappropriate, to cry and yell and accuse God of not acting in ways we need God to act. But it is the evidence that we trust that God is all in on redeeming all things, and a commitment to meeting divine determination with a full-life determination of our own.

Lament Is Political

One of the staggering heresies that has wormed its way into the church, perhaps more common in some Evangelical traditions but not unknown in mainline ones, is the idea that naming the pain and brokenness that so many suffer within the current order of things is somehow at odds with the Way of Jesus. Whether it is written off as "woke," or just overly sensitive, or inappropriate for church, or too divisive, or too political, if we cannot lament the state of things in church—if we cannot name injustice, if we cannot call unrighteousness what it is, if we cannot voice our own pain and take seriously the pain of others—then we will have a hard time getting near the One who is near to the brokenhearted. If we cannot weep in the presence of God, we will have a hard time following the One who openly wept over Jerusalem, and the death of his friend, and the mess of the world.¹⁰

It is true, though, that lament *is* political; in that, the critics are right. It is political because it shapes us in particular ways and develops a kingdom of God conformed posture towards the world, in all its mess and wonder.

---

9. Andy Crouch argues convincingly that algorithms pose some of the greatest danger and hindrance to Christian spiritual formation. Comer and Crouch, "Luminary Interview."

10. Luke 19:41; John 11:35; Matt 26:38.

If we believe that the world is headed towards redemption, that in the life, death, resurrection, and reign of Jesus, we have a clear sense of God's purposes for all creation, then we are right to lament and resist the ways in which we are not there yet. If we have a sense of the beauty of creation, the miracle of humanity, the gift of love, the abundance of life for which we are made, then the ways in which all these things are mangled and marred ought to break our hearts.

There are at least two reasons that many expressions of church are not very good at lament—or even unwilling to entertain the possibility of it. The first is a theological or biblical error. We have over-emphasized Paul's instruction to rejoice in the Lord, while ignoring his insistence that we bear one another's burdens and weep with those who are weeping.[11] We have shied away from books like Job, or Lamentations (except, maybe, the middle of chapter 3), or the psalms that are a little too intense, imagining that if we are faithful then everything will be all good.[12] We have assumed that confidence in the promise that "all things work together for good for those who love God" means that when things go sideways, or we admit that all is not well, then our love of God is in question.[13] In many cases, we have been more deeply influenced by the promises of free-market capitalism that all pain can be mitigated by our best efforts and our personal resources, than by the Way of the Savior who knows our weakness and takes it seriously.

Which leads to the second challenge for the church that would lament: many congregations are made up of the relatively affluent and comfortable, and we have appearances to keep up. Or, like me, many of us tick all the obvious boxes of privilege, and so lament seems somehow inappropriate. What do we really have to complain about? The best we can often come

---

11. Gal 6:2; Rom 12:15.

12. Churches that follow the Revised Common Lectionary may find themselves even more hindered in lament, because the readings so often skirt around the truly hard stuff. For instance, when we come to a reading like Ps 137, we only make it to verse 6. The part that really opens us up to lament, the bit about dashing our enemies' babies off rocks (ultimately a prayer that the injustice and violence would end with this generation), we get squirmy and give up. But what about the times when we actually feel that way, when we harbor unspeakable feelings towards those who have wronged us or others? If we cannot voice that stuff to the One we can trust to exercise justice beyond our capacity, then we simply carry it around, and as often as not it finds its way out of us in ways that are every bit as destructive as the things we hate. If we do follow the Lectionary—and there are good reasons to do so—then we might consider boldly including the parts it leaves out and seeing if we can wrestle a blessing out of them.

13. Rom 8:28.

up with is sympathy or guilt. We feel badly for those who are suffering and vaguely guilty that we benefit from the systems that cause the suffering of others. I may be a touch cynical, but it often feels like when the church gets close to lament, we end up mired in self-serving mollification. We know that good people should feel badly about bad things, so we name that and move on. We are always susceptible to virtue signaling. We pray that God would do something, with no expectation that God might use us in answer to our prayers. Or we acknowledge our complicity in injustice, apologizing ad nauseam, but never getting beyond apology to actual reconciliation—a strategy that temporarily soothes guilt, while keeping us in positions of power and privilege. We center our own feelings and wonder why the plight of others is not addressed.

This is not to say that our feelings do not matter if we happen to be people of privilege, simply that sadness and guilt are not lament. Lament is deep and transformative. It is an act of resistance and a form of resilience—a refusal to be conformed to the patterns of this world, by the renewing of our minds and the transformation of our lives.[14] For those of us in mainline, European-descended, culturally privileged traditions, we would do well to learn from communities who have had to develop a powerful practice of lament. That is one way to renew our minds and resist the systemic injustices that distort humanity. I am grateful for writers and prophets like Cole Arthur Riley, a modern-day psalmist, who invites us to attend to the voices of others, "never overpowering them, but following in solidarity," even when their experience is not ours.[15] The Black church has a long and painfully necessary history of lament as an act of honesty and resistance, a way of naming the way things are and refusing to submit to the malformations of a fallen world. Among oppressed peoples, lament is a practice that moves individuals and communities beyond the empty promises of optimism and into a thick and determined hope.

That said, lament is not a spiritual cure-all. It is one of the resources we have for speaking truth and making space to rest in it. And truth-telling is not always a means to happiness, but it might be a signpost on the narrow road to deep and lasting joy, but it misses the easier way of temporary good feelings. The psychiatrist Curt Thompson reflects on the challenges of one of his patients facing the truth of her own brokenness and the distorted narrative that shaped her life in the world. On the one hand, naming truth

---

14. Rom 12:2.
15. Riley, *Black Liturgies*, xvii.

allows us to turn from distortion. But on the other hand, doing so is not for the faint of heart:

> Only now, she found that the very turning revealed a weakness in her swim stroke, given how long she had been swimming in agreement with the old narrative. To swim against that current was to suffer. Suffering as one who is practicing living in the age to come, while the present age is passing away, trying to take her with it.[16]

To lament in honesty and resistance is to open ourselves up to suffering: suffering as those who, in the grace of Christ, have caught a glimpse of the world as it will be when God gets what God wants, but as a result are deeply aware that the world is not that, yet. Unfortunately, to live fully and freely in the world, as the children of God and ambassadors of heaven that we are, is to refuse to deny that suffering.[17] As followers of the One who will not run from the cross in fear but runs towards it in faith, we are called into the love that empties itself for the sake of the world, and that will not choose a more efficient, less costly way.[18]

I recall listening to a young woman who had been widowed not long after she was married. She spoke about how, in the depths of her grief, she heard Ps 23 again, for the first time. She was confronted by the line "even though I walk through the valley of the shadow of death, you are with me." Suddenly, she was struck by the frustration of the main verb in that sentence: *walk*. She was eager to get through her grief, get around some of it, if possible, and run through this season as quickly as she could.[19] But there is no running through death's valley—trying to will only lead us to trip and fall in the darkness. The only way through is to walk it, trusting in the One who is not only with us, but also leading us to the other side. Trust in God does not make the valley any less traumatic or painful or scary, but it does allow that we are not alone, and we are not doomed to walk in the shadows forever, long as they may be.

In the psalm, the valley is sandwiched between the lush fields and cool streams to which the Shepherd leads his flock and the banquet table that the Lord prepares, even in the presence of our enemies.[20] The three images

---

16. Thompson, *Deepest Place*, 99.
17. 1 John 3:2.
18. Phil 2:5–11.
19. I cannot remember where I heard this story. I can only appeal to Scripture and say, "someone, somewhere once said . . ."
20. I have often wrestled with that image, wondering what the presence of enemies

are inseparable, giving us a vision of the way things are meant to be, the way they often are, and the way that they will be again. If we allow for only one or two, we miss the fullness of the gospel. But held together, the pasture, the valley, and the banquet keep us weird in the world. We will learn to live as those who know that "the Lord is close to the brokenhearted, *and* saves those who are crushed in spirit," trusting with our lives that "none of those who take refuge in God will be condemned."[21]

Lament Is Presence, Not (Only) Solutions

I have often joked that other peoples' problems are easy to solve. It's not true, of course, but we tend to have a sense of apparent clarity about how to improve the lives of others. When it comes to others, what decisions should be made, strategies employed, and actions taken can seem straightforward. Unfortunately, I have not always known that this is not true, and in some cases have done more damage than good, offering what I thought were solutions but turned out to be platitudes at best and downright ignorance at worst. I trust that I am not alone in wanting to solve problems for friends and family and people who show up to my study wondering what on earth is going on in and around them. Even with the best of intentions, more often than not problem-solving is a strategy for avoiding lament. It is a way of running through the pain of a situation, rather than fixing our eyes on the One walking us through it. Not that there are never answers to problems. But we are culturally conditioned to look for the quick fix, which often results in cosmetic solutions to deeply disfigured realities. It's just more efficient than the deep work that leads to healing and life.

When it comes to lament, it is easy to underestimate the value of companionship and community, folks who are willing to get into it with us and with whom we are ready to labor in prayer and pain. For any number of reasons, many of us tend to want to keep our brokenness to ourselves and the brokenness of others at arm's length. But it is important to remember that the psalms that lead us so intentionally into lament are, first and

---

means, especially for those of us who have an expansive confidence in the saving work of Jesus. What are our enemies even doing there? Is this an opportunity to one-up our enemies in heaven? Or are we looking towards the day when we will sit at table with those who have harmed us, finally in the reconciling light and presence of God, together? On my braver days, I hope for the second option.

21. Ps 34:18, 22, italics added.

foremost, liturgical prayers, meant to be prayed by a worshiping community. Praying the hard ones together allows us to join our voices with those who are suffering, even when we are not, without imposing our words or feelings on them. And when we are suffering, to hear our pain voiced by a congregation can make space for us to be seen and known and cared for, to allow others to bear our burdens with us.

I have heard or read the parable of the good Samaritan countless times and heard almost as many sermons on it.[22] But only recently did someone point out to me the fact that once the Samaritan bandages the man left for dead and loads him on his donkey, he takes him to an inn and stays there with him overnight, tending to his wounds.[23] The Samaritan had the resources to outsource that care. We know as much, because eventually he leaves money behind for the brutalized man to be nursed to health and promises more when he gets back. And who would have blamed him? He is clearly on his way somewhere. But it matters that the initial act is full of presence—tangible, intimate presence. Money alone will not do the work of healing. Practical responses will not be enough to restore dignity on their own. Swooping in to save the day cannot be neighborly in the way of heaven's kingdom. Only the Samaritan's willingness to be interrupted and his patient, personal attention can reach and begin to heal what has been truly damaged in the roadside mugging.

As those learning to live into our image-of-God status, in the world as it is, for the sake of how it will be, we cannot ignore the closeness of God when it comes to the brokenhearted. We must take seriously God's willingness to receive prayers of lament, to hear the cries of his people, to respond in kind when we seek to draw near to God's divine shelter. If God draws close to those who are crushed in spirit, so must we. And given that God's pace always defaults towards patience, so should ours.

I have long been struck by a story that Parker Palmer tells in his book *Let Your Life Speak*. He reflects on a season of deep depression, a time of total disconnection from others, his true self, with God. It was a prolonged stretch of despair, during which many friends and acquaintances offered advice designed to bring him through to the other side—often in ways that made them feel better, deflecting his pain rather than engaging it. In contrast to that, he writes that,

---

22. Luke 10:25–37.

23. This insight came from the Sanctuary Mental Health Course, "Session 5: Companionship."

> Blessedly, there were several people, family and friends, who had the courage to stand with me in a simple and healing way. One of them was a friend named Bill, who, having asked my permission to do so, stopped by my home every afternoon, sat me down in a chair, knelt in front of me, removed my shoes and socks, and for half an hour simply massaged my feet. He found the one place in my body where I could still experience feeling—and feel somewhat reconnected with the human race.
>
> Bill rarely spoke a word. When he did, he never gave advice but simply mirrored my condition. He would say, "I can sense your struggle today," or, "It feels like you are getting stronger." I could not always respond, but his words were deeply helpful: they reassured me that I could still be seen by *someone*—life giving knowledge in the midst of an experience that makes one feel annihilated and invisible.[24]

I am staggered by Bill's patient generosity, his unwillingness to rush through the pain that his friend was feeling, and to simply offer himself in the void of depression. So often, healing begins in letting our lament be seen and heard, to be joined in the discomfort and agony by someone, or some community, who will resist the temptation to solve the problem, in favor of finding the place where we can still feel the experience of connection with our humanity. Of course, the need to lament and clinical depression are two different things, but the experience of disconnection and dehumanization overlap.

Because of the potential for disconnection, it is worth acknowledging that like any spiritual practice, there is always a danger that lament can get twisted towards some end that is other than God's. It is entirely possible to get so caught up in the mess of the world, or our particular circumstances, that we are insufficiently aware of what is happening in our particular corner of it. I am convinced that it is a demonic strategy to overwhelm and paralyze us by the things we cannot affect, so that we are distracted from the things we can. Evil is every bit as satisfied with spiritual paralysis as with indifference. We are no closer to the kingdom of heaven when we are glued to our news feeds than when we turn a blind eye to the suffering of those right in front of us. To be people who love like Jesus loves and heal like Jesus heals means primarily attending to the people and places that God has entrusted to us and called us to steward.

---

24. Palmer, *Let Your Life Speak*, 63–64.

The love of Jesus is love that loves what's right in front of it. Mercifully, God has everything in view. We can narrow our focus. To do so does not mean we do not care about the serious problems of the world, the systemic injustices, racism, sexism, poverty and homelessness, on and on, that plague our cities and countries. We do. We must. And, we must not allow the overwhelming challenges of the world to distract us from loving who and what is right in front of us. Ours is a God who refuses, again and again, to love generally. The God we know in Jesus is relentless in loving specifically, intimately. And so, as we look to the restoration of all things, let us not overlook the opportunities that we have been given to be agents of love and peace and healing and hope wherever we are and whomever we are with. It is one of the ways that we can connect not only with the humanity of others, but with our own.

Lament Is a Way of Life

It is a paradox that the way of lament can lead us in the way of abundant life, by the simple and gracious fact that true lament brings us into the presence of the God of life. It brings us into the company of the One who tames chaos into beauty, who creates in delight, and whose commitment is to the flourishing of life. Lament expands our vision to understand that what is happening here and now is of cosmic value, *and* whatever is going on will not get the last word on us. What is good is a shadow of things to come. What causes suffering is doomed.

I have never risked using St. James's thoughts on suffering in a pastoral situation. I don't have his guts. He writes:

> My brothers and sisters, whenever you face trials of any kind, consider it nothing but joy, because you know that the testing of your faith produces endurance; and let endurance have its full effect, so that you may be mature and complete, lacking in nothing.[25]

I have never suggested that someone should delight in their suffering because it is probably making them stronger or more resilient. The reason I think James can get away with it is that he is radically committed to the way of the cross, in a way that I am still aspiring to. He understands that following Jesus will often put us at odds with the world, and, in the context James and Jesus occupied, people who opposed the ways of the

---

25. Jas 1:2–3.

world—which is to say, the Roman Empire—ended up on crosses.[26] For James, some measure of suffering and discipleship were inseparable. The relative ease of Christendom was a long way off. The first-century church was learning how to be a community of resistance to the violence, greed, and power-mongering that were, and are, so opposed to the Jesus inaugurated kingdom of love and justice and righteousness. James is not talking about the suffering that comes with the loss of a loved one, or a terminal diagnosis, or the breakdown of a relationship. He is talking about the inevitable suffering that comes when we draw close to the heart of God, who longs for the healing of this broken and beloved world.

On this side of Christendom, although we are far from persecuted, even as the church has found itself decentered from public consciousness and places of power, we are again in a time when the church has a chance to be a peripheral community of resistance against the things that distort our humanity, destroy the earth, and keep us and our neighbors from flourishing with spiritual fruit. We have a chance to let our witness to the ways and means of God be costly, in a way that invites others in and which was sometimes a less dynamic option when the world assumed the church's authority. Martyrdom may always—dare I say, should always—be on the table, but it seems unlikely for most of the Christians I know. Yet we are still called to a kind of willful suffering—not masochism, but a downward mobility that brings us alongside the brokenhearted, where God is, that we might be lifted from the ash heap together. When that happens, we bear witness to God's future that is pulling us towards itself.

Pastor Jon Tyson adopts the phrase "A Creative Minority" from the late Rabbi Lord Jonathan Sacks to think about what the church is or can be in the increasingly secular world in which we find ourselves, especially in North America.[27] This calls to mind Jesus's image of the church as a bit of yeast that leavens the whole batch, or the tiny seed that produces a remarkable harvest.[28] To be the church as a creative minority means taking seriously Jesus's countercultural call, in as many creative ways as possible. Of course, anyone who makes a go of creating something opens themselves up to suffering. There is risk and challenge, fear and an inevitable moment when it is not at all certain that the vision can come to life. Following Jesus

---

26. See Miller, *Witnesses of These Things*, for a longer reflection on Jesus's call to take up our crosses.

27. Tyson and Grizzle, *Creative Minority*, 7.

28. Luke 13:18–21.

in the places we find ourselves may not literally cost us our lives—though there are many places in the world where it could—but it may cost us the lives we have been taught to want, or the respect of neighbors, even relationships with family. We may be asked to give up things we have worked hard for, or to radically rethink the purpose of things that matter to us. We will be called to learn to love our enemies and pray for our persecutors, to care for the poor and folks we would rather do without. We may be asked to leave our proverbial nets on the shore and follow Jesus into something entirely unexpected and possibly undesired.[29] And with call to sacrifice, and radical love, and a new direction can come a deep sense of loss, or uncertainty, which can drive us into lament as easily as the pain of the world. We might as well be honest about the fact that we have had our hearts set on things Jesus may not be that interested in. He tells us that no one who gives up everything will fail to get abundantly more (also some persecutions), but we are allowed to allow that giving things up with purpose is still a loss.[30] The Way of Jesus drives us into the complicated blessing of community, sacrificing the illusion of autonomy and the comforts of self-centered individualism.

And yet, if we will do it, if we will be attentive to the Spirit and faithful to Jesus, caught up in the redeeming, restoring, renewing ways and means of God, we will discover that the other side of loss is life. We will discover a hope that is only possible in the company of the God who made all things and is making all things new, and those caught up in that newness, learning to be shaped by it. In that hope, we develop the resilience to move through despair and lament, into the life we are made for. Norman Wirzba puts it like this:

> Authentic hope takes courage and perseverance as people commit to changing the contexts that generate despair. The philosopher Jonathan Lear has called this kind of hope "radical hope" because it signals a commitment to work for a world that often exceeds anyone's current ability to understand it, and a resolve to work for a future that in many of its details remains unknown. This form of hope requires a creative imagination to picture what currently seems like an impossible future, and it requires a committed heart that does not easily give up when obstacles to the realization of this future emerge. When hope takes this radical form, grief and lament are not forms of resignation in the face of this world's pain

---

29. Mark 1:16–20.
30. Mark 10:29–31.

and violation. They are, instead, forms of power that fuel a person's commitment to "join with all the living" and offer a healing hand of help.[31]

There is a persistent biblical confidence, rooted not in our best efforts but God's faithfulness, that "those who go out weeping, bearing the seed for sowing, shall come home with shouts of joy, carrying their sheaves."[32] In Jesus, we have seen just how far God will go to be with us and for us, that God will cross heaven and earth to find and restore us, and that having loved us, he will love us to the end.[33] And even the end is not the end for the God who raises the dead. We risk lament because we know Jesus meets us there. And we rejoice because he refuses to leave us there. We lament because the world is a mess and so are we. And we rejoice because, even now, all things are being made new.

And so, this benediction from Cole Arthur Riley rings true:

> Go in freedom, with tearstained cheeks and stability of heart. Feel deeply and honestly, without being consumed. And may God hold fast to you if the tide of despair strengthens its pull, that you could grieve with the gravity you deserve. *Amen.*[34]

---

31. Wirzba, *Love's Braided Dance*, 13.
32. Ps 126:6.
33. John 13:1.
34. Riley, *Black Liturgies*, 94.

Signpost 6

Freedom

Here, Christendom's decline is the church's gain. The loss of Christianity in the public square that many bemoan today actually gives us the opportunity to reclaim the freedom to proclaim and demonstrate the truth of the gospel in a way we cannot when we try to serve the nation as one among many helpful props of the state.[1]

The Lord redeems the life of his servants; none of those who take refuge in him will be condemned.

PSALM 34:22

Freedom Is Weird

ONE THING THAT MAKES freedom weird is that it is a notoriously slippery word. It is something we all assume is a natural good, for which we are made. Politicians talk about it. Banks promise it. Car companies appeal to it to sell the newest models. Social media influencers insist we grab at it. We enshrine freedom in our national anthems and put it on our currencies. We go to war for it and save our money for it. For some, freedom is the right to do whatever we want, whenever we want to, or to say anything without consequences. For

---

1. Hauerwas, *Jesus Changes Everything*, 127.

others, it has to do with the way we express ourselves in the world, or what we believe and how we worship, or with whom we are intimate.

Most often, it seems, we imagine freedom as the absence of restrictions or impositions. We want free markets, and free speech, and free expression, and freedom of religion. To be free is to be unencumbered by boundaries or barriers. "For freedom, Christ has set us free!" proclaims St. Paul, which sounds very much like the Way of Jesus is the way of uninhibited self-expression.[2] Because of Jesus, we can do anything we want! "All things are permissible but not all things are beneficial" seems to be the primary caution: as long as it is beneficial, we are good to go.[3] Only, how do we determine what is beneficial? Is a Christian approach to freedom "If it makes you happy, go for it"?

Clearly not. But this points us to the strangeness of Christian freedom, the weird way that followers of Jesus understand what it means to live fully and freely in the world. Christian freedom is not only, or even primarily, freedom from anything. Of course, we trust that it is freedom from sin and guilt, freedom from death, freedom from the things that bind and weigh us down. But mostly, it is freedom for something. Paul continues his reflection on freedom for his Galatian congregation in a way that might make our heads spin. "For you were called to freedom, brothers and sisters, only do not use your freedom as an opportunity for self-indulgence, but through love become slaves to one another."[4] What?!

Christian freedom is not freedom from restrictions; it is freedom for something. It is freedom to love God, and the things God loves with everything we've got. It is freedom to have the same mind as Christ, who had everything and gave it all up for more, for love's sake. For us. Christian freedom is not simply the elimination of boundaries; it is freedom to live and move and have our being in the broad space of God's grace.[5] It is to learn that we will never reach the edges of the height, depth, length, and width of God's love for us in Christ, and to be invited into a similar way of love in and for the world.[6] Christian freedom is the freedom to be nothing less than we are created to be, trusting that God has been forming us since the

---

2. Gal 5:1.
3. 1 Cor 10:23.
4. Gal 5:13.
5. Ps 18:19.
6. Eph 3:18.

very beginning,[7] with purpose and passion and a divine determination that our lives are sufficient to bless the world, to embody the commonwealth of heaven.

In a sense, true Christian freedom requires a commitment to all of the signposts for strangeness that we have considered so far: worship, prayer, incarnation, discipline, and lament—practices that form us as followers of Jesus, not just pursuers of personal happiness. Christian freedom necessitates a self-surrender, trusting that God really does know us and love us better than we do ourselves. It is to learn from Mary to say, "Let it be with me according to your word," and from Jesus, "Yet, not my will but yours be done."[8] It is a cultivated readiness to let God's kingdom come and the desires of God's heart take shape in every aspect of our lives. The conviction of saints in every generation is that if we cannot do that, we are not yet as free as we are made to be. If we are resistant to letting God's ways and means have priority in all we do, then we are not free from God's desire, we are just bound by our own limited wants, needs, feelings, and vision.

One way that followers of Jesus push ourselves and each other beyond our own limited desires and understanding is to be relentlessly communal. Community is essential for true freedom because it bridges the space between public and private. Wendell Berry contends that there are things that we assume are profoundly personal, but can only be properly understood communally. For him, case in point is sex. We, in North America, currently live in a culture that assumes that what we do with our bodies (especially if those bodies happen to be white, male, and fully able) is entirely up to us, or ought to be. There can be no restrictions on what we do with our bodies or with whom. Except that, if we understand ourselves to be fundamentally relational beings (and there is no other biblical framework), that cannot ultimately be true. We are incarnate beings, in relationship, so how we use our bodies, for good or ill, is not only a matter of private discernment.

Nor is it a matter that can be adequately addressed in a typically public way. We see this in the fraught and contentious ways that issues of sex and sexuality are often battled over in the public sphere and in the church. Irrespective of what the given issue is, most often one side of the conflict wants to restrict and control what can be done with our bodies, for one reason or another, while the other side wants to insist that anything other than absolute individual autonomy is an assault on our essential personhood.

---

7. Ps 139:1–18.
8. Luke 1:38, 22:42.

In either case, our bodies tend to be reduced to units of production and objects to be consumed. We are not well served by trying to discern what it means to be embodied, sexual people in the broadly public or explicitly private sphere. Berry argues that "the indispensable form that can intervene between public and private interests is that of community."[9] Community overcomes the impersonal generalizations of public dictates and invites us to understand ourselves not as isolated individuals but humans in relationship. We may find some of Paul's directions about how to comport ourselves in sexual relationships a little grating to our modern sensibilities, and he is unavoidably a product of his time and place. But the reason he can weigh in on these things with authority—especially as an unmarried celibate—is his conviction that what he does with his body is every bit as important to the community as what any member does. The things he says are not necessarily proclamations for all times and all places, even if some are certainly worth taking seriously in this time and place. But they are evidence of a community working out a sexual ethic that bore witness to a different way of being in the world, a different way of honoring bodies and dignifying individuals than the culture around it—a way coherent with the Way of Jesus and the kingdom of God.[10] Our task is no different.

Of course, sex is low-hanging, if tantalizing, fruit for thinking through the fact that our freedom is properly worked out in community. We could just as legitimately consider how we are with our money, how we respond to violence, how we establish justice or deal with conflict. None of these things can, or should, be restricted to one-size-fits-all public answers, or reduced to matters of personal choice, opinion, and practice. Unfortunately,

---

9. Berry, *Sex, Economy, Freedom and Community*, 119.

10. Some of the more challenging passages in the New Testament have to do with the determined relationships between men and women, particularly husbands and wives. We bristle when Paul says something like "wives, submit to your husbands as to the Lord" (Eph 5:22). There are a number of reasons that might set off alarm bells, but one reason is that over the history of the church we have stopped at the instructions to wives and ignored those to husbands. When Paul tells his congregations that husbands do not have authority over their bodies, but their wives do, he is undermining a whole host of contextual assumptions about the Roman household. What is more, that he so regularly addresses women directly—not to mention children and slaves—is in itself a radical choice. He would have been perfectly within his rights to address the men in the room alone, as they held the legal and household authority. We may not always like what Paul says, but that he says anything plants the seeds for a more equitable future, which we are still attempting to live into. Our modern sensibilities, morals, and ethics did not develop in a vacuum, but they are the long result of generations of people discerning how we can live well together, and for Christians, how we can live Christianly together.

this also assumes a degree of vulnerability that is neither easy nor often encouraged. In order to nurture communities in which we can help one another navigate the complexities of life together well, we must develop a willingness to engage in deep, mutual care for one another. To borrow a few of Paul's phrases, we have to learn to bear with one another, to consider the needs of others above our own—which is only life-giving if others are willing to do the same for us.

This mutuality highlights one of the inherent risks of church. To say that our freedom is for others can be a way of restricting actual freedom, when being for others becomes a requirement, explicitly or implicitly. Communally shaped freedom only works, only brings life, if the expectations are the same for all members, in terms of mutual submission and care. We have seen the damage done when one person or a handful of people get to dictate the terms for everyone else. Consistently, the pastors in Scripture insist that positions of authority are not about power but about service; that the least among us should be treated with even greater reverence; that those of high station should rejoice in downward mobility, while those who are lowly should experience the community's uplifting.[11] How we are with each other, how we exercise our freedom in the name of Jesus, is going to look very weird in contexts where we are regularly encouraged to believe that our own self-improvement, security, and pleasure are our highest goal. A truly Christian community is about more than the people one attends church with—though, hopefully not less. A truly Christian community will be made up of people of every age, stage, persuasion, and position willing to wrestle with and for each other, until each is blessed, and together we are conformed not to the pattern of this world but the age to come. A truly Christian community will strive, in every aspect of its life together, to be weird enough in the world as it is, that when God gets the world God wants, we will fit right in.

I have often been intrigued by communities that are sometimes called New Monastic Communities. These are not monastics in the traditional sense of the word, those who live in a monastery together, sometimes more or less separate from the world around and committed to strict Rules of Life, under the authority of an abbot or abbess. Instead, they are geographically connected individuals and families, some who share living space, others who live on their own, who have covenanted together to live in particular, formative ways. They do share in a Rule of Life that structures

11. Jas 1:9–11.

their collective use of time, energy, and resources, as well as shapes their commitments to the locality that they find themselves in. But they spend their days living in the world like the rest of us, going to work and school, raising kids and caring for neighbors. Many move to what they call "the abandoned places of the empire," in order to work with those already there for renewal and restoration.[12] While this is not a calling for every Christian, this grassroots movement towards an embodied, communal commitment to giving witness to God's coming kingdom has important things to teach the wider church. Their weird determination to live differently is a testimony to what is possible when Christians come together, pay attention to the Way of Jesus, and determine to live it out together.

Freedom Is Political

Of all our signposts, freedom feels the most obviously "political." Perhaps because the idea is so regularly invoked by heads of state and local politicians, or because it is so closely tied to national and civic identity. In democratic societies, our constitutions and laws, our systems and institutions are all ostensibly designed and committed to ensuring and protecting the rights and freedoms of individuals as we have collectively determined them. Yet, for all the talk of freedom, it seems to be a precarious reality: if we do not up military spending, or uphold these rights and limit those ones, if we do not vote for this party, or adopt this economic system, or keep that other country in its place, or express ourselves in particular ways, then our freedom is suddenly in jeopardy. It always seems to be in danger of being taken away. Which suggests that it is not a particularly robust state of being for many of us, no matter our position or privilege.

One of the more pointed Christian convictions, shaped by the biblical witness, the communion of saints, and the ongoing work of the Holy Spirit, is that our freedom is never truly in jeopardy—no matter what is going on in the world around us. For instance, we may have deep concern about the way the Bible talks about slavery, and it is incontrovertible that the biblical communities existed in a context in which slavery was an accepted reality. Even so, one of the ways that the early church began to undermine the institution of slavery was by assuming the humanity and dignity of slaves, addressing them as humans and not property, and insisting that their actual freedom was not tied to their specific station. It could be argued that

---

12. Wilson-Hartgrove, *New Monasticism*, 39.

acknowledging the position of slaves as assumed and accepted kept oppressed people down, and certainly those parts of Scripture which ought to have been liberating have been used many times since to justify the restriction of freedom for, and abuse of, particular peoples. For those of us in European-descended traditions, that is an argument we must take seriously; we must reckon with our historical complacency and ongoing participation in systems that benefit us at the expense of others.

Still, it seems quite clear that within the framework of the nascent church, coming to life in the long shadow of the Roman Empire, local communities of Jesus followers were reorganizing their collective lives in a way that must have begun to transform how they understood their mutual connectedness and freedom.[13] They insisted that whatever their station in a household, they had one common Lord, and his example was to be followed, his loving authority submitted to, by both those with the most power and those with the least.[14] These little house churches spent their Sundays embodying another way of relating to one another that was not based on the hierarchical and dehumanizing systems that governed the world as they otherwise knew it. To share in worship, prayer, meals, and sacraments across social boundaries must have had a profound effect on the ways in which they interacted with one another and with their pagan neighbors when they returned to the rest of their lives. Together, they were embodying a fresh possibility, rooted in the inherent, God-designed freedom of each person. We have known some of the fruit of those first seeds. Much of the harvest remains to be seen, even in cultures where slavery is technically illegal.

The thing that compelled the church then—and ought to compel the church still—to live in ways both mutually submissive and ultimately freeing was not any contextual political system, but a cosmic one. It stemmed from the basic conviction that Jesus is Lord. The church, at its best, is

---

13. The survival of the institution of slavery as a key element of empire building is at least in part the lamentable result of the church's eventual collusion with worldly forms of power. The conversion of Constantine in the fourth century and the Christianization of the Roman Empire radically altered the ways in which the church functioned and structured itself. Christendom, the (often) nominal Christianization of the Western world with the blessing and support of the empire, cannot be said to be a universally bad thing. But on the other side of it, it is easy to see the ways in which the state had a much more significant, and deadly, influence on the church than the other way around. I tend to agree with others that our current position on the margins of society rather than in the seats of power is a much more effective place for us to be formed in and committed to the subversive Way of Jesus.

14. Eph 6:9.

constantly working out the implications of our belief that in Christ we see the lengths to which God will go to love this world, that every person we meet bears the image of God, and that there is nothing that God will not give to see that image restored where it is marred. We are constantly working out our conviction that the One who insists that it is the poor and the pure, the peaceable and the persecuted, the meek and the mourners and the merciful, those hungry and thirsty for righteousness—flourishing and fruitful relationship with God, our true selves, each other, and creation—those are the ones to whom God's kingdom belongs.[15] We are learning to embody our conviction that the One who sits on heaven's throne is the One who teaches us that the first will be last and the last first, that those who would be great by heaven's metrics are the servants, the ones who are committed to the love and nurture of others.[16] We know that we fall short in all of this, sometimes catastrophically. We know that Scripture has been used in violent and oppressive ways, ways that make some wonder if it can be of any good use at all anymore. And yet, like that early and fumbling church, we are called again and again to reclaim and proclaim the truth that whom the Son sets free is free indeed.[17]

As David leads us in our Song for the Strange, Ps 34 culminates in the promise of redemption: the promise of a freedom we cannot claim for ourselves and which no one can take away. David frames this redemption as both a finished and future reality. The finished is that "the Lord redeems the life of his servants." That is what God does: God sets free, present tense. There is freedom immediately available to us in the love of God, the grace of God, the presence and consolation of God, the sure and certain knowledge that God's desire for us is good. When God determines to do something, it is effectively done, even if we await its ultimate fulfillment.

And we do. We wait and we long for the renewal of all things, the freedom we are made for, sometimes with groaning and weeping. It is a telling thing that in St. John's vision at the end of Scripture, amid the heavenly worship, the joyful songs of praise, remains the saints' cry: "How long, O Lord?"[18] There is still a considerable portion of our lives lived in the hope that "none of those who take refuge in [God] will be condemned."

---

15. Matt 5:1–11.
16. Matt 20:26.
17. John 8:36.
18. Rev 6:10.

Nevertheless, Christian hope, and the life that hope engenders, is rooted in the conviction that ours is a God who makes promises and keeps them. That coming day of renewal is as certain as if it were already here. And so, we live towards that. We live now for the day when all people will be free, when every tear will be wiped away and every hungry belly filled, and creation restored. As we are being formed in the Way of Jesus, we learn to live with our neighbors, as though they are the very people Jesus would give everything to set free, because he has. We learn to live within systems that are dehumanizing and designed for the wealth of some, as though the day is coming when everything that hinders the flourishing of life for all people will be destroyed, because it is. We learn to resist the rhythms and requirements of our culture that keep us from loving each other, ourselves, and creation well. We learn to store up treasures that last—the things that lead to love and justice, wholeness and beauty—worrying less and less for the stuff that rusts and rots and fades away.[19]

Although my bias is towards the local and particular when it comes to the life and work of the church, being in cahoots with Jesus, whose love is for the world, means that while we do the sometimes hard work of loving what is right in front of us, we do not do so without developing a commitment to freedom in every corner of the world. Working for freedom and justice is a spiritual gift that is basic to the life of the church; it is walking in step with the Spirit of God. Like any spiritual gift, it may take different forms. There are those whose minds and hearts are specially tuned to the plight of folks far away, or the larger systemic changes that need to be made in our own countries, and those who are zoned in on more local and immediate need. The church needs both voices. As those in the thick of justice movements are wont to point out, until everyone is free, none of us truly are. Here, Paul's vision of the church as a body is important.[20] Understanding the church not as a series of independent communities but a global body can help to expand our vision and heighten our concern for the ways in which God's kingdom is taking shape and being hindered in places very different from ours.

Of course, we should not be worried only for the freedom of Christians in other countries, but remembering that the church is there, hopefully working out what it means to follow Jesus in those contexts, is a way for us to avoid too narrow a vision of what God is up to in the world. It is a

19. Matt 6:19–21.
20. 1 Cor 12:12–31.

way for us to feel ourselves connected to people and places we do not know and may never see. And with that sense of connection, we are empowered in different ways to support the work of freedom wherever it is happening. I was grateful, a while back, to have Andrew Larson come share his work with our community. Andrew is a remarkable man who is working with the organization Nea Zoi (New Life, in Greek), a Christian community working in Athens, Greece. Athens, as a port city, is a major hub of human- and sex-trafficking in Europe.[21] Andrew and his team live and work among the people, mostly women, who have been lured or taken, often from places of poverty around the world, and brought to Athens as products of a sadistic, inhuman business. Nea Zoi works carefully and surreptitiously to build relationships with these women, support them and—in the best cases—establish a plan to get them out, and set them on the road to freedom. It is slow, dangerous, and sometimes nearly hopeless work, with people who have been brutalized in countless ways. The number of women they are able to get free from these conditions in a given year can often be counted on our fingers.

And still, their work is a testimony to the world that is coming, a refusal to shrug their shoulders and abandon those who are least and lost in the eyes of the world as it is. Without Andrew's testimony, I would have had no idea about life in Athenian slums. But now I do. And I have a wider—and more challenging—vision of what God is doing in one faraway place. With Andrew in mind and prayer, while his is not my calling, his witness can shape the way that I work for the freedom of those among whom I find myself—both those strangled by the "lures of wealth and the cares of the world" and those run over by the systems obsessed with those lures and cares.[22] His testimony reminds me that in Jesus's name, we are free to be bound by the love, grace, and call of God for the world God loves.

Freedom Is Presence
(As We Are, for the Way We Will Be)

The way we throw the word around, freedom sounds invariably easy, an unlimited spaciousness to do as we please. Hard-won, perhaps, but once we have it everything is smooth sailing. But again: Freedom as it is often used tends to be understood as freedom from something—whether tyranny, or

21. https://www.neazoi.org.
22. Mark 4:19.

restrictions, or poverty, or external responsibility. For those of us who follow Jesus, our freedom is always *for* something. Freedom in the Way of Jesus is much closer to what we often imagine as discipline—and likewise, Christian discipline is much closer to freedom. It is entirely true that whom the Son sets free is free indeed, but that same Son turns to us and says, "As the Father sent me, so I send you." We are freed not for self-indulgence, but to become who we are created to be. We are free to claim our identity as children of God, and coheirs with Christ, with all the rights and responsibilities of representing God's household in the world.

There are any number of ways that we might reflect on what it means to become who we are created to be, that is to be fully human, fully alive. But we would be hard-pressed to do better than the two-part creation poem we call Gen 1 and 2.[23] The opening pages of Scripture are where Christians develop an imagination for who we are and our proper work in the world. We see, first, the priority of God in all things. The God who proceeds in gentleness and joy to call all of creation into being. The story of all things begins with a creative outpouring, a universe positively teeming with life, as God's Spirit shapes chaos into beauty. It is important that unlike other ancient creation stories, the physical world is not the result of a war between gods, or made for the purposes of serving the gods. In fact, there is no particular reason given for God's determination to make night and day, earth and sky, land and water, every plant and animal. The cosmos is not the result of divine strife or need, but it seems simply to be God's delight. There is nothing necessary about what is, except that the Maker of heaven and earth wants it that way. And the way it is, is good. Very good. That is the world into which we and every living thing are birthed.

We should not rush past this opening fact, that we are a part of this creation that need not be, but is, and is full of wonder and mystery and beauty, everything shot through with divine intention and love. If we can wrap our minds around that, and let it sink into our hearts, it will change the way that we live in the world. We cannot help but be attentive, caring, and delighted with creation if we pause regularly to consider the absolute and holy miracle of the world that we find ourselves a part of. I wonder if that is something like what Paul meant when he said that "all of creation

---

23. In what follows, I am assuming a degree of familiarity with Gen 1 and 2. I will not cite every reference, but I would invite anyone who needs a refresher to pause and read these two chapters.

waits with eager longing for the revealing of the children of God."[24] All creation is desperate for us to recognize who we are, because until we do so we will continue to believe that we are hopelessly dependent upon economic and political systems that are destroying people and the planet for the sake of profit. Genesis 1 gives us an opportunity to reimagine how we are made to live, not as relentless consumers, but ambassadors of God's goodness and beauty-making. We too often act as if we are somehow separate from the rest of creation, that its lot is not also ours. But that is the kind of wishful thinking or willful ignorance that is making this world increasingly uninhabitable for millions and millions of people.

We are intricately woven into the fabric of creation, completely dependent and interconnected. We may have an important role, to which we will turn presently, but it is an important part of the story that we do not even get our own special day of creation; we and the animals all show up on day six, together. That said, Gen 1 and 2 also shape an imagination for not only our place in creation, but, even more, how we are meant to live in creation. We are placed in the garden to "till and keep it." To tend to it. To do the work of co-creating and maintaining the conditions for everything else to flourish. We may have a certain power over the plants and animals, the soil, but we are ultimately servants of these things. Even as we are told to "have dominion" over every living thing, we would do well to recognize that "dominion" comes from the Latin word for "Lord." For those of us committed to the lordship of Jesus, how we exercise dominion must be reflective of his will and way—a willingness to love, even at deep, personal cost, for the sake of the other.[25] We are not owners of creation; we are its God-imaged stewards. If we bear God's image as the poem insists, then we also share in God's self-giving concern for all things.

That concern is a partnership between ourselves, God, and each other. Creation is relentlessly relational. The more we learn about plants and animals, soil and water, the more we understand the intricate web of relationships that make for flourishing life. Given this, we should assume that any proper care of creation will be relational. And, since we are inherently a part of creation, we too need to be cared for relationally. It is not good for us to be alone, as God so succinctly puts it. We need each other, we need

---

24. Rom 8:19.

25. Many commentators have noted that the Hebrew in Gen 1:28 suggests not a dominance, but a loving care for all of creation. In the Hebrew Scriptures, to have authority over things—like a household, for instance—is not about personal power, but the expectation of generous care. We are always blessed to be a blessing.

connection to God as the source and sustainer of life, we need the wild web of everyday miracles that make the sun shine and grass grow, the inconceivable number of atoms working together to form every blessed thing, the impossible precision of earth's tilt and atmosphere.

And all of this is meant for joy, for a tireless and beautiful freedom to live, move, and have our being as part of creation, stewards of its gifts, in partnership with one another and our God. One of my favorite images in the whole story is of Adam and Eve, naked and unashamed. That is freedom. Perfectly known, vulnerable, loved, and alive in the world. In order to embrace that kind of freedom on this side of Eden, we need to develop practices of presence with God, ourselves, each other, and creation. We need to cultivate the conditions that make for life, for us and other—spaces where we can be truly known, where we can deal with shame and its distortions, and where we can grow into our truest selves—agents of the love that made us, redeemed us, and is making us whole.

Freedom Is a Way of Life

There is an astonishing scene in the television series *The Handmaid's Tale*, based on the dystopian novel by Margaret Atwood, at the end of season 2, episode 2.[26] June, the main character, is on the run from the authorities who have taken control of a portion of the United States, following a civil war. Those who emerged victorious have established a regime that subjects its population to inhuman, surreal restrictions and brutality, based on a restrictive (and, I would argue, heretical, piecemeal) reading of Scripture. June is hiding out in the headquarters of the former *Boston Globe*, where those who have sought to silence any dissenting voices have clearly massacred journalists and shut down the paper. In an act of resistance, she begins to collect items left at desks—pictures of family, shoes, a Red Sox cap, drawings by children, a Pride flag. And she creates a shrine with these traces of the past. She uses pictures and stickers, kids' art to cover the bullet holes in a wall, which, along with a line of nooses, are the only remaining evidence of what has happened, of those whose lives have been cruelly taken. Having covered the evidence of state-sponsored barbarity, she kneels, lights candles, arranges the mementos of those slain, and prays: "God, by whose mercy the faithful departed have found rest, please send your holy angels to watch over this place. Through Christ, our Lord, amen." Her prayer is

26. Barker, "Unwomen."

based on the standard Catholic graveside prayer. That, it seems to me, is an extraordinary image of resilient freedom, even in the shadow of terror and extreme violence.

Of course, *The Handmaid's Tale* is fiction, though art often reveals things truer than we have the courage to admit. There are elements of the story that are painfully close to current political events, in countries around the world. June consistently represents a strength necessary for true faithfulness: a deep unwillingness to cave to the powers that are determined to stifle life, even when they claim to be doing it for the sake of a greater good. Although she is, by any worldly measure, a prisoner, she is resolute in her claim to freedom. Her prayer, in the shell of a decimated newspaper building, comes as something of a surprise in the arc of the story, and it lays bare the reality that true freedom is not contingent on circumstance. True freedom sometimes looks like a prayer at a gravesite.[27]

Freedom, in the Way of Jesus, is a deep, sometimes absurd commitment to the gospel promise that there is nothing in heaven, earth, or hell that can outstrip or outlast the love of God, and God's determination to crush the things that would crush us. Nothing that steals, kills, or destroys life will define us in the end—it will not even register a comment. No place is ever ultimately God-forsaken, no person hopelessly lost. Freedom is buoyed by a hope rooted in an empty tomb and empowered by an ascended Savior. It is growing in the knowledge that those two realities—the resurrection and the reign of Jesus—form the boundaries of our lives.

How that looks in practice may be as varied as the number of people willing to get after it. It requires discernment, a diligent attention to our contexts, and a readiness to take the people and places around us with the same seriousness as Jesus does. There is nowhere in our lives where the twinned hope of Jesus's resurrection and reign cannot be lived out. The one thing Jesus's resurrection and reign cannot do, if we will be faithful, is get mired in theological abstraction. I appreciate Tish Harrison Warren's work of imagining the daily details and monotonies of life as acts of liturgy, forms of worship and attention to the ways and means of God, a willingness to

---

27. There is a painful moment, later in the series, when June prays that God would "help me forget me" (Skogland, "Other Women"). This is the inverse of the freedom she displayed in the face of death and a striking reminder of what is at stake when we talk about true freedom. June's prayer here is the opposite of the prodigal son's moment of "coming to himself" (Luke 15:17), remembering who he is, to whom he belongs in the truest, freest sense. Freedom is rooted precisely in knowing and remembering who and whose we are, and living from that, whatever else is going on.

allow even the most minor parts of our day—making the bed, or brushing our teeth—to be covered in the grace and goodness of Christ.[28] Perhaps what is most insightful about her work is the fact that it is often the people, places, and things closest to us that we are most likely to forget have something to do with God. It is easy to imagine that great acts of justice, uncommon expressions of love, places exotic and other than ours might be shot through with God's glory. It is harder to imagine that changing the baby's diaper, or vacuuming the floor, or guiding teenagers, or managing employees, or the park up the street or the pub on the corner are entirely within God's view and worthy of divine concern.

I love to play pool. I can happily do it for hours. I am decidedly average, but there is something about the game that pleases me deeply. I even delight to play with people much better than me, losing every game, if it means an afternoon of practice and the occasional improbable shot. The pool table has often been a place where I meet the most unlikely people. As a university chaplain, pool at the local pub has sometimes been a way to make connections I never would in a sanctuary, or sitting at a booth in the student union building under the banner of a religious club. I remember when I did a ministry internship in a small town in New Brunswick, one of the first things I noticed was that it had a pool hall. The only problem was that I was told, on my first official tour of the town, that under no circumstances should I be seen coming out of there. It was not a place for a minister. I wish I had more guts at the time. I never did go in. Although these instructions were given out of concern for my station in the community, a place that had more conservative Baptist churches per capita than anywhere I had ever been, they were misguided. This advice fell under the restrictive assumptions that nothing that goes on in a pool hall is of gospel concern, and no Bible believing Christian should be caught in there. I wonder what opportunities I missed to build relationships with folks who would never darken the door of the church. Even if I did not manage to share the gospel with them, might I have opened a way for the next person? Or might I have simply learned something deeper about the needs, hurts, joys, and loves of the people who lived in the town in which I was supposed to be growing as a pastor? Might I have encountered Jesus in a way I never could in more appropriate company? Gospel freedom means that we are open to the experience and expression of God wherever we are, without restriction or fear.

28. Harrison Warren, *Liturgy of the Ordinary*, 25, 37.

Of course, we are every bit as likely to miss out on what God is doing in places much less sketchy than the local dive bar. The annoying kid in our classroom, the boring bit of administration, the mind-numbing daily commute, making dinner *again*, Saturday chores, all of these things—along with every other blessed thing we do—can be places of divine encounter, opportunities to take seriously the miracle of the person in front of us, and tend to the needs of the contexts we find ourselves in. Every place, every person, every moment is an invitation to work out what it means to receive the gracious freedom of God to resist the stuff of death, literal and figurative, and to live towards the abundant life for which we and all things are made. Activist and organizer adrienne maree brown is exactly right when she contends that the way we are in the small things—the local, the particular, the personal—models and precedes anything we hope for on a large scale. She says, "it was and is devastatingly clear to me that until we have some sense of how to live our solutions locally, we won't be successful at implementing a just governance system regionally, nationally, or globally."[29] As we think about what it means to be free in the Way of Jesus, and to live towards the way things will be when God gets what God wants, we must begin to work out the realities of resurrection and ascension right where we are.

Again, how that will look will depend entirely on where we are and whom we are with. It will be different in a rural setting than in an urban one. It will be different for those who are navigating life as a single person than for those figuring it out in the complexities of family life. It will be different for those with significant financial margin, or clear authority, than for those living closer to or on the edge of things. It will be different as a young person, trying to discern the path that will hopefully stretch many years into the future, than for those of us in middle age, or those who have a lot more years behind than ahead of them. Although the call to love God and neighbor with everything we've got is baseline for Christians, there is no set pattern for how that is lived out. But one thing is for sure: The call to follow Jesus is full of both comfort and conviction at every age, stage, and station. We can never avoid the challenge of Jesus, the disrupting and disorienting way in which he leads, subverting our closely held convictions about the way things are. We can be sure, however, that when we enter into Jesus's disruption and disorientation, we will also receive, many times over, his comfort and consolation, the perfect freedom of his love and mercy.

29. brown, *Emergent Strategy*, 52.

In a sense, it is freeing to know that the call of Jesus is not a call to blind conformity. Jesus takes us seriously, even if there are some things that we can confidently say will mark a deepening discipleship. For instance, anyone growing in faithfulness to the Way of Jesus will necessarily be growing in the Fruit of the Spirit. When we come under Jesus's apprenticeship, we will become more loving, joyful, peaceful, patient, kind, generous, faithful, gentle, and self-controlled. Those are growth metrics of faithfulness, the things that seed God's kingdom in and through us. Again, there is not a single aspect of spiritual fruitfulness that can be lived generally; it all takes shape in our lives, particularly.

That is incredibly freeing, and also potentially overwhelming and guilt-inducing. How can we know and accurately measure our growth if there is not a clear, universal grading system? The first response to any such anxiety is to remind ourselves that we live and are saved by grace. Jesus sought us out long before we thought about following him. He gave everything for us, knowing exactly who we are, before we knew anything of him. So, we take a breath. We are not earning anything. We are growing into a reality that is already established, not trying to create something by our own best efforts. Jesus lives and reigns whether we get it right or not; his resurrection and ascension are not contingent on the quality of our actions, or the depth of our belief, if we have any at all. And, fortunately, there are time- and saint-tested practices that can help us become more and more attuned to the reality that our souls most deeply long for, that can help us participate in the world that we are truly made for, even as it is coming to life—even when we can hardly see it at all.

One such practice is known as the Daily Examen. This is a prayer practice described by St. Ignatius of Loyola in his *Spiritual Exercises*, in the sixteenth century. There have been many variations on the Examen in the centuries since Ignatius began to teach his followers to pray in this way, but they all follow a basic pattern:

- **Stillness**: finding space to become aware of God's presence.
- **Gratitude**: reviewing the day, giving thanks for what has passed (this practice is best done at the end of the day, but choose your own adventure).
- **Reflection**: paying attention to feelings that arise as we reflect on the day, and then noticing when we were in step and out of step with God's Spirit and the Way of Jesus.

- **Prayer**: praying our feelings, offering them all to God, paying special attention to any laments and hurts, or any place we feel called to confession and repentance.
- **Hope**: looking towards the day to come, in hope and trust, committing ourselves to God.[30]

Whether this form of prayer or some other means of attention and reflection, a practice like it is essential for discerning the ways that Jesus is guiding us and the ways in which we need to repent, turning to reorient ourselves to his path. Practiced over time, the anticipation of reflection will make us more immediately aware of our feelings and responses in real time, helping us move in the freedom that we are made for. It makes that possible because we are more and more aware of the ways in which we miss the opportunity to take St. Paul's commission seriously, to do whatever we do, in word and action, in the name and Way of Jesus, to the glory of God.[31] That may seem impossible, and in a sense it is. But it is not meant as an unrealistic expectation that will mire us in guilt and failure. Instead, it is a conviction about our truest selves, the things we are actually meant for: We are people who are created in such a way that we can glorify the Maker of all things, the King of kings and Lord of lords. Paul is taking us much more seriously than we tend to take ourselves, believing that in the light of the resurrection, by the power and presence of the Holy Spirit, and under the Lordship of Jesus, we can actively participate in the redeeming, renewing, and sustaining work of God.

The commission to do everything we do in the name and Way of Jesus is also why Christ's ascension is so integral to a Christian imagination not only about the world and where it is headed, but about who we are. If Jesus sits on the throne of the universe, then we are not subject to the demands and whims of those who would have us live for something other than God's glory, anything less than the Fruit of the Spirit in all we do. As with just about everything in a Christian life, this is easier to say than to do, and even Paul freely admits that he falls well short of the mark.[32] When my blood sugar dips or my favorite sports team plays poorly, or any other trivial thing upsets the way I think things should be, I am deeply aware of just how far I

---

30. A quick internet search will bring up countless resources for Ignatian prayer. For variations on the Examen: https://www.ignatianspirituality.com/ignatian-prayer/the-examen/#variations.

31. 1 Cor 10:31.

32. Rom 3:23.

have to go, if I'll do everything for God's glory. Nevertheless, as we discern the ways that we will spend our days, how we will be in work and leisure, what gets our energy and resources, the promise that the only one truly worthy of the title *Lord* has called and claimed us is perfect freedom to let all that we are and have bend towards the beauty that God is, even now, making out of the chaos of the world. We are never as trapped in a situation as we might feel. We are never reduced to what others think of us or expect of us. We are never limited to the most we can muster up or defined by that nagging inner voice that says we're not good enough. We are children of the Most High, siblings and coheirs with the King of kings. We are free indeed.

The World God Wants
The Way of Jesus

> Let the same mind be in you that was in Christ Jesus.
>
> PHILIPPIANS 2:5

> Long ago God spoke to our ancestors in many and various ways by the prophets, but in these last days he has spoken to us by a Son, whom he appointed heir of all things, through whom he also created the worlds.
>
> HEBREWS 1:1–2

Jesus Is Weird

JESUS IS NOT A signpost on the way to the kingdom of God; he is the kingdom of God embodied, he is the clearest glimpse of the world as it will be when God gets what God wants. As the preacher of Hebrews puts it, we do not see everything we are hoping in, but we do see Jesus.[1] And Jesus is wondrously weird. He consistently eludes our expectations, resisting all efforts to pin him down with doctrine, or confine him to a polite, Christian corner. He speaks in ways that make even his closest followers' heads spin. He does things that confound our cleverest strategies for success. He regularly says things that, instead of drawing crowds, make people back away slowly, if not turn and run the other direction. While we may recognize that he has the "words of eternal life," it is hard not to be sympathetic to those who

---

1. Heb 2:8–9.

think he may be a little off.[2] It may feel heretical to say that Jesus is weird, but the Gospels are relentless in making clear that he will not conform to the demands of the world around us. Unless we confront that fact and let it shape us, let his way hold sway in our lives, we are doomed to committing ourselves to an idea of Jesus that fits within our limited understanding, rather than following the One who leads us to abundant life.[3]

One of my favorite instances of Jesus's weirdness happens in the middle of Luke's Gospel. In chapter 15, we have a series of well-known and beloved parables: the parables of the lost sheep, the lost coin, and the prodigal and his brother. Each of these draws us into the extravagant grace of God for every one of us—the God who seeks out and saves the lost, who yearns for our return and rejoices when we who were dead are now alive, we who were lost are found. But then in chapter 16 we hear Jesus tell his disciples—not the gathered crowd, interestingly—the parable of the dishonest manager, the hero of which is a household manager who squanders his boss's property. When he is caught and called to account, he then rips the rich man off further by reducing the debts of those who owe his boss, so that people will like him and welcome him into their homes when he is fired from his job—because he is self-admittedly "too weak to dig, and too proud to beg." Jesus ends this story saying, "And I tell you, make friends for yourselves by means of dishonest wealth so that when it is gone, they may welcome you into the eternal homes."[4] What are we supposed to do with that?! Is that a word of eternal life? I have preached that parable several times, and I am not at all sure that I have gotten it right.

Which is at least part of the point: Jesus is not a test we can study for. Together, the Gospels of Matthew, Mark, Luke, and John are a trustworthy guide to following him, but they are not a textbook with all the answers. Jesus will not be reduced to religious information. As we have seen at each Signpost, the Way of Jesus is relentlessly personal, relational. The only way to know him is to get into his holy mischief, to join him in righteous disruption, to let him disorient us from the ways of the world so that we can be reoriented by the *renewing* of our minds, not just the improving of them.[5] The parable of the dishonest manager—or truly, any of Jesus's parables, if we are paying attention—makes clear that following Jesus, apprenticing

2. John 6:66–67.
3. John 10:10.
4. Luke 16:9.
5. Rom 12:2.

under him so that we can do what he does, will demand a readiness to take every situation, every place and person, with the same kind of seriousness that he does. There are no easy answers, only faithfulness that makes us weird in the world.

Of course, it is not only Jesus's cryptic teachings that are weird, but many of his straightforward instructions send the mind reeling. His instructions about forgiveness or generosity, enemy love or financial planning in the Sermon on the Mount are enough to make most of us second-guess signing on to his mission. We cannot help but wonder how we are supposed to live out the Sermon and make our way in the world. Mercifully, we do not have to wonder long; we need only watch and learn, as he does it—and then trust that he means it when he says that those who love him will do what he does, *and even greater things*.[6] We are made, individually and collectively, to join in Jesus's strange and enlivening way: to be salt that adds holy flavor to a sin-bland world and light to illumine eyes dimmed by the way things are—flavor and vision that signal another way.

We unquestionably need another way. It is broadly acknowledged that, at least in North America, although we are in almost every way richer, healthier, better educated, and safer than people have ever been in history, we are less happy and more anxious, depressed, and fearful than our ancestors. We face social breakdowns, environmental disasters, economic injustice, on top of a frenetic pace of life, an epidemic of loneliness, and systems that demand allegiance by fear and intimidation. What kind of savior would he be, if Jesus was satisfied with the status quo, or a bit of an improvement on the way things are? The best news we have is that Jesus is determined to make all things new. Even if his call unsettles or scares us, our souls long for another possibility than we are so often offered. Into that longing Jesus says, "Come, follow me; learn from me."

Heeding that call may cost us everything that we have been taught matters, but it is the way into what truly matters. It allows us to move freely in the way that we are made to, nimble in love, graceful in mercy, strong in peace, tenacious in hope, trading anxiety for trust and disintegration for wholeness. And when we do that, when we give up the stuff that binds and weighs us down for the easy yoke of Christ, we will be weird in the world.[7] We may find ourselves in conflict with our culture, at odds with those who will dig their heels into the world as it is. But at least as often, if not much

---

6. John 14:12, italics added.
7. Matt 11:28–30.

more often, we will embody an alternative that captivates a weary world. Consider the holy circus that was the early church.[8] Caught up in the wild freedom of the Spirit, they began to live in a way that looked like Jesus—full of healing, generosity, freedom, and joy; lives that looked like the opening of our Song for the Strange, the uninhibited praise of God echoing in everything they did. And folks could not get enough. They had the good will of all the people. Every day, the Lord added to their number those who were being saved. Every day, people signed on for a new way.

The Way of Jesus is weird, but it is stunningly beautiful. I have long loved the well-worn story of the Samaritan woman at the well, from John 4. It's a marvelous conversation between Jesus and a woman of (apparently) ill-repute, in which all manner of social boundaries are transgressed. One of the more delightful parts comes when Jesus tells the woman, who has come to get water for the day, that he has water that will quench her deepest thirsts forever. It is a metaphorical water, of course. He says, "Everyone who drinks of this [well] water will be thirsty again, but those who drink of the water that I give them will never be thirsty. The water that I will give will become in them a spring of water gushing up to eternal life."[9] The word translated as "gushing up" is the Greek word *hallomai*, which is much more often used in reference to people leaping, jumping, or dancing. It is the word that describes the response of those who are healed of infirmities that kept them mat-bound, as they experience the wonder of new strength and possibilities.[10] That is the unexpectedness, the weirdness, the liveliness that we are meant to embody as we make our way through the world. That is the beauty we get to make known as we align our lives with Christ—with Ps 34 in our bones—as our lives magnify the Lord, as we exalt his name, bearing witness to the love we have come to know, as we taste and see the goodness of God more and more.

Jesus Is Political

The kingdom of heaven is the heart and total of Jesus's life and mission. It is the content of his first sermon and the subject of his parables. Its reality is the basis of his response during his trial, as he lets Pilate know that his

---

8. Acts 2:42–47.
9. John 4:13–14.
10. For instance, Acts 3:8, 14:10.

kingdom is "not from this world."[11] When he is hung on the cross, he dies under a sign that says, "This Jesus, the King of the Jews."[12] When he is raised and ascended, the preacher of Hebrews tells us that he "sat down at the right hand of the Majesty on high."[13] When St. John catches a glimpse of heaven, he sees Jesus, the slain Lamb who roars like a lion, seated on heaven's throne, determining to make all things new.[14] That Jesus is political, relentless in the gathering of a people for the sake of a holy revolution in the world, is biblically undeniable. The question for those of us who would follow him is not whether we ought to be political *as Christians*—many do not want to mix faith and politics, for good reasons—but how should we be political? What does it mean to pledge allegiance to this king, to say that Jesus is Lord, and Caesar is not, as the church has been saying since the very beginning.[15]

Perhaps the most important thing to consider as we ask that question is the fact that readiness for the kingdom of heaven requires repentance. Repentance means turning around, a radical change of mind. It means consciously choosing a different way, going a different direction than we have been heading. When Jesus comes Spirit-launched out of the wilderness, preaching, "The time has is fulfilled, and the kingdom of God has come near; repent and believe in the good news!" it is a call to action, a call to live and move and have our being in a new and life-giving way.[16] As we follow Jesus through the Gospels, answering that call, we learn quickly that the way in which we will be formed for the kingdom of heaven, shaped as the *polis* for a world-made-new, will not be the way of power grabbing, violence, and control that our world is used to and for which far too many Christians are making headlines. Instead, the one who will be great is servant of all.[17] Getting in on the kingdom of heaven requires downward mobility, not becoming great in the eyes of the world's power brokers, but becoming childlike.[18] It requires a simplicity of heart, curiosity, wonder, and playfulness, a willingness to be led where we may not much want to go. It requires acknowledging our needs and dependencies, knowing that we

11. John 18:36.
12. Matt 27:37.
13. Heb 1:3.
14. Rev 21:5.
15. Claiborne and Haw, *Jesus for President*, 16.
16. Mark 1:15.
17. Mark 9:35.
18. Matt 18:3.

cannot make it on our own. It means following the One who is worthy to be called King of kings, because though he was equal with God, he did not consider divine power and authority worth clinging to but emptied himself for love's sake.[19]

Too often we have used the name of Jesus to baptize the world as we are familiar with it, the world we know how to navigate by strength and determination. In direct contradiction to the teachings of Jesus, the church has regularly been at the forefront of empire building, claiming divine authority to avoid self-giving love and grabbing all we can at the expense of others. In the wake of Christendom, we may no longer have the kinds of cultural power that allow us to do that anymore, but we must always be aware of the temptation to claim Jesus for our causes or desires, before those causes and desires are conformed to his will and way. We easily forget that we belong to him, he chose us, he called us, not the other way around. At the end of the day, his call is what it always has been: *repent and believe the good news, then come follow me*. We, every bit as much as the first disciples, must tend to the ways that Jesus's call challenges our closely held assumptions about the world and our place in it. Until that day when the glory of the nations will be marched into the City of God, and every death-dealing thing left outside its gates, we are called to be that creative minority, working for new life in the shell of the old.[20]

King David, in Ps 34, leads us into the presence of the One who makes the humble radiant, whose goodness is intimately knowable, who is generous and abundant, who moves us to flee evil and seek good, who draws near to the brokenhearted, who rescues, redeems, and avenges those run over by the world. That's how this king points to *his* Sovereign, which tells us much about what it means to be politically committed to the ways and means of God. Any community we form, any system we implement, the ways in which we interact with the world around us must be in line with God's concern for the poor, radical generosity, mutual intimacy, oriented towards abundance rather than paralyzed by scarcity. We must be people who create space for the healing of broken hearts and bodies, where crushed spirits can be revived, a refuge for those battered by the storms of life. We must be people of redemption—those working for the freedom of others, even as we learn to live into the Christ-wrought freedom that is ours. There may be countless ways that these things play out, ways in which we work the

---

19. Phil 2:5–11.
20. Rev 21:26.

things of God into our daily lives so that they can flow into the lives of our neighbors. One thing is certain, though: the ways and means of God throw a wrench into many of the machinations of the cultures in which we find ourselves. Karl Barth puts it this way: "The church exists to set up in the world a new sign which is radically dissimilar to the world's own manner and which contradicts it in a way that is full of promise."[21] The call of Christ is as revolutionary now as it was when he first began gathering people into the kingdom of heaven movement.

The circumstances may be very different for us than for those first followers or the early church. In the relative ease of post-Christendom, martyrdom is much less likely for us than for those who first walked the Jesus Way. We are more likely to be ignored, or shunned, than seriously persecuted. Even so, we are still sent out "like sheep into the midst of wolves," and so must learn to "be wise as serpents and innocent as doves."[22] I think it is quite a fun thing that Jesus sends us out to be wise as serpents: crafty, mischievous, wise in the ways of the world, only towards the world as it will be when God gets what God wants. When Jesus tells the parable of the yeast, of a woman who sneaks yeast into a batch of dough, the word he uses there which we translate as "hid" or "mixed" is *egkruptō*, from which we get the word "encrypt."[23] There is a kind of intentional hiddenness about the way that we are meant to smuggle the kingdom of God into the kingdoms of the world. Discipleship is sometimes a covert operation, but instead of infiltrating to do damage, we are surreptitiously loving, working undercover for the flourishing of the world. We are to be innocent as doves, which is to say perfectly aligned with the kingdom of God. Obviously, we are not to be always sneaking around, or silent in our commitment to the things of Jesus, but perhaps these images can give us a sense of excitement or playfulness in the ways that we seek to bear witness to the hope that we have. While there are times that we must speak with determination and clarity, how might we also sneak a little more gospel into an office, a kid's sports practice, a courtroom, or a boardroom? Not every situation is a time to preach. Sometimes we gotta be a little craftier than that.

In the end, to say that the Way of Jesus is political is to appeal to our imaginations for the multifaceted ways that we are able, as we are and with what we have got, to give full-life expression to our commitment to God's

---

21. Quoted in Tyson and Grizzle, *Creative Minority*, 15.
22. Matt 10:16.
23. Matt 13:33.

oncoming kingdom. How can we organize our lives so that they are naturally spacious, and welcoming soil for the Fruit of the Spirit? How can we create systems in our churches and in our communities that foster radiance, and renewal, and refuge? What practices do we need to embed in our daily routines, and what do we need to let go of or weed out, so that we can be both as wise and innocent as Jesus would have us?

Jesus Is Present

Christians say and believe a lot of weird things. But right up at the top of the list is our conviction, rooted in a lived experience, that Jesus is immediately present with us and to us, through the Holy Spirit. When he promises that where two or three of us gather in his name, he is there with us, we take that promise seriously.[24] When he says that we are sent as agents of good news, to baptize and disciple in every corner of the world, and that as we go, he's going with us right to the end of the present age and into the next one, we trust that he means it.[25]

To many in mainline traditions like my own, it may seem a little far out there, a bit too "holy-roller," to say that Jesus is, in a literal sense, with us. However, if we fail to attend to these promises, or resist the imminence and intimacy of the Holy Spirit, we underestimate the means we have at our disposal for living out our discipleship, and once more we risk confining Christian faith to an idea to be assented to, or a theological theory. But when we recognize the presence of Jesus in every moment, closer than our next breath, then we know that St. Peter is right when he says that we have been given "everything needed for life and godliness, through the knowledge of him who called us by his own glory and goodness."[26] Jesus will not ask us to do anything that he has not done, nor will he send us to do anything for which he will not also equip us, *by his own glory and goodness*. We have everything we need, to do what we are made to do, which, in turn, allows us to take seriously that we are sent as he is sent, to do what he does.[27] When we understand that, then we cannot help but recognize that he, and therefore we, are always and only sent *into* the world, for its redemption. Eugene Peterson's rendering of John 1:14 is poignant: "The word became flesh and

24. Matt 18:20.
25. Matt 28:20.
26. 2 Pet 1:3.
27. John 20:21.

blood and moved into the neighbourhood."[28] Whatever we believe, pray, sing in church or in private devotion, gets lived out in flesh and blood in the neighborhood. All the faithfulness and hope, the healing and mercy we proclaim in Christ, the wild love of God is meant to find local shape, in our bodies, homes, workplaces, schools, everywhere we spend our days.

There are any number of practices and disciplines that can help us develop an awareness of Christ's presence with us and attune us to the guidance of the Holy Spirit. One that many people find helpful is Centering Prayer, a meditative practice that moves us towards union with God.[29] Some people find this kind of prayer difficult, as it requires stillness and quiet, which can be elusive for both internal and external reasons. Nevertheless, it is a practice that stretches across Christian history and which assumes that we are meant to be intimately present to God, naked and unashamed, as Genesis puts it, with the Lover of our souls.[30] Sadly, in many Protestant traditions, the idea of mystical union with Christ is regarded with deep suspicion, which is indicative of our default to intellectualism. Intellectually robust faith and theology are a gift to the church, but on their own, they leave us with the impression that the Christian life is more about having the right information than about a life-long formation in the Way of Jesus. We need spiritual intimacy with God, in Christ, and by the Holy Spirit, because the nature of discipleship is relational. Jesus's first disciples would have spent nearly every moment with him, in constant presence, learning his rhythms, absorbing his teaching, asking questions, integrating his way of being into their own. Very little of what they learned would have been through explicit teaching, compared to what was passed on through mutual presence. The result of that intimacy was a group of people, largely uneducated, relatively powerless, run-of-the-mill people, who turned the world upside down.[31] They did not do that because they had the right answers. They did it because the kingdom of God was coming alive in them, in the presence of Jesus and the power of the Spirit. That same intimacy and power is available to us and necessary for us if we will do our part in turning the world as it is upside down—which is, in the end, right-side up.

---

28. Peterson, *Message*, John 1:14.

29. For instructions on the practice of Centering Prayer: Contemplative Outreach, "Centering Prayer Method."

30. Gen 2:25.

31. Acts 17:6.

This intimacy is all over our Song for the Strange, as David calls us to the God whose praise and name is constantly in his mouth and on his lips, whose salvation is tangible and experienced in every corner of life, whose commitment is to drawing near and providing refuge. We cannot pray with David and come away with a purely rational faith, or an easily explainable experience, any more than we can accurately explain what it means to be in love, or the feeling of being in the presence of overwhelming beauty. This is a God who invites us to taste and see divine goodness, who delights in full-body worship, who longs for our faces to be turned towards him that we might reflect the radiance in which we are made. If, as the preacher of Hebrews says, long ago God spoke through prophets like David who made the word of God present and powerful, in these last days, that word comes to us as a Son, made flesh and blood and moved into the neighborhood, inviting us to experience his goodness and glory, so that we can be radiant in the world.[32]

Jesus Is Life

"I came that they may have life, and have it abundantly."[33] That's Jesus's promise, his mission statement, his way of describing the kingdom of God for each person: life and more life. The challenge for us is to allow that the conditions for that life are set, in his life, death, resurrection, and reign. Christianity is not a strategy to get the life we want, so that now all we have to do is follow a series of steps and it can all be ours. Instead, the daily work of discipleship is to learn to live in the light of resurrection, trusting that there is nothing in us or in all creation that can separate us from the love of God in Christ Jesus our Lord, because the maker and sustainer of life is on the throne of the universe.[34] Our job is not to "make a difference" in our lives or in the world, but to live in the difference Jesus has made.[35] Our task is to develop an embodied imagination for what Jesus means when he says that he is the vine and we are the branches, who will produce the fruit of heaven's kingdom. We need an imagination for what he means when he invites us to abide in him, knit together so intimately that it is as if we are

32. Heb 1:2.
33. John 10:10.
34. Rom 8:38–39.
35. Hauerwas, *Jesus Changes Everything*, 131.

one plant, one body.[36] The branches on a vine do not make a decision to be there; they grow naturally out of it. The branches are not responsible for creating the conditions for their fruitfulness, they simply respond to a reality that pre-exists and sustains them, because that is what they are made to do. Likewise, we, who are grafted into Christ by the grace of God, are meant to be so deeply connected that we naturally produce the fruit of the kingdom—that is the goal. The life we are created to live, the life our souls deeply long for, is not somewhere else, on the other side of our best efforts. It is life lived in the nurture of the vine and care of the vinedresser.

There is a breathtaking, divine vulnerability in the image of a vine and its branches. It is as if Jesus is saying that the fullness of the kingdom cannot come, or will not come, without us—which is not to overstate our own importance or underestimate God's capacity to bring about whatever situation God wants to bring about. Instead, it is incredible to know that Jesus invites our fruitfulness, not simply his own. He is the vine, which by itself is incomplete. Without branches to bear fruit, the life of the vine is nothing like what it is meant for. A fruitless vine might be decorative, but it is not much use otherwise. Jesus willingly risks that, calling us to play our part in bringing to life all that God wants for this world. God will not simply impose the divine will on the world, but God works in and with us for the flourishing of life. The inverse is true, as well. Branches disconnected from the vine eventually wither and die, which means that we cannot live the life we are made for if we are disconnected from the source of that life. A branch cannot produce the fruit it longs to detached from the nourishing root system, the vine that delivers nutrients from the earth and supports its growth.

This is an integral image for discipleship, as we learn what it means to produce the first fruits of a new creation, to participate in the abundance Jesus wants for us.[37] It points us to both the source of our life and work, and it imbues all our days with beautiful possibility. There is growth to happen in this day, fruit to be produced that only we can produce; there is meaning and purpose to each moment. There are also seasons of abundance, and seasons of fallowness. A branch that produces constantly would consume the nutrients necessary for true fruitfulness, what is needed for the good stuff worthy of the wine at heaven's banquet. We need times when the vinedresser prunes us, getting rid of what is unhealthy or worn out, and making room for new growth. But whether we are in a season of production or a

---

36. John 15:1–11.
37. 1 Cor 15:20–23.

season of rest, we are integral to the life of the vineyard. We have a part to play in the harvest.

What is more, a branch's fruitfulness is never simply for itself. Even if we can imagine the branch delighting to produce fruit, freely and naturally doing what it is made to do, perfectly at home in the joy and beauty of creation, the fruit is always for the nurturing of another—or to make more fruit. As we are fruitful, we image the source and sustainer of our lives; we become those who bear the seeds of new life, new fruit; and we live lives that provide sustenance and beauty and holy flavor in the world. Our lives can be the means by which others taste and see the goodness of God. How, in our everyday lives, are we bearing the seeds of new life? How are we nurturing those around us, providing the literal and spiritual nutrients that support life? How are we allowing ourselves to be nurtured towards that end? How are we maintaining our connection to the vine?

Like any of our Signposts, our sustained connection to Jesus is easier talked about than lived. There are any number of situations, concerns, and people eager to lop us off the vine. We are easily distracted from what is truest about us and this world, by relentless entertainment and creeping anxiety. Sometimes we are simply too pragmatic for our own good. We are totally susceptible to the temptation to believe that our branches can last on their own, can produce fruit without abiding in Jesus, especially for those of us who spend our days under the easy illusion that our lives consist mostly in what we do, what we are able to build for ourselves, and what we can sustain on our own strength. I have often said that it is hard to be a Christian with a credit card, because credit cards give us the impression that we are self-sufficient. We can solve our own problems, provide for ourselves, respond in cases of emergency. But the myth of the self-made and self-sustaining human falls flat much more assuredly than it proves true. We inevitably run up against our creatureliness—which, when we recognize our connection to the vine, is a great gift, much less so if we find ourselves shrivelled on the ground.

However, even when we do find ourselves worn out by our own efforts, at least part of the hope of Christian faith is that while we certainly have a vinedresser who prunes away what is fruitless, tossing it on the burn-pile—every flourishing vineyard needs that—we also know that, in God's vineyard, the resources for life and new life are wildly more than we can ask or imagine. What looks shrivelled and hopeless to us is full of possibility for God. Ours is a hope rooted in resurrection, the sure and certain promise that life is going to win, that death's sting has been neutralized for good. Again, we may not see that clearly, yet, but we do see Jesus. In company with this God, in life with the True Vine, there is nothing so lost that it cannot be found, nothing so dead that it cannot be made alive. That is the hope in which we stand, the hope with which we move into the world, trusting in the One who is willing and able to do abundantly far more, in us and through us, than we can yet see, by the presence and power of the same Spirit who raised Jesus from the dead.

Epilogue

SOME OF THE WRITING of this book happened during the church season of Lent. I do not always take something on, or give something up throughout Lent, but this year I wanted a way to mark the season and to deepen my discipleship. I decided to wear my clergy collar every workday. In my tradition, as well as many other Protestant expressions, many clergy do not don the symbols of our office, and I rarely have over the years since my ordination. The collar is eschewed by some because of its past association with power, authority, and privilege, which are so often at odds with Christian faithfulness and practice. For some, in an eagerness to flatten church hierarchy and celebrate the "priesthood of all believers," decreasing the distance created by visible accoutrements of ordination is worth foregoing them. But these days, the collar is weird, more than anything.

I had two curiosities as I began to wear it regularly. The first was how I would be received, both by strangers and acquaintances—folks on public transit, cashiers, baristas at my local coffee shop, or the receptionist at the gym, some of whom may have some idea what I do for a living but mostly chose to forget as soon as they found out. It has been somewhat anticlimactic. I do catch people on the bus looking at me a little longer than they might otherwise have, or more familiar people doing a double-take. Catholics receive me with more honor than I am used to, but otherwise, people do not seem all that interested.

The second curiosity was how I would respond, and whether I would feel like I needed to modify any behaviors when I was much more clearly representing the church, no longer in incognito mode. I am glad to know that the experience has not been much of a big deal for me either, any more than for others. However, there is something about the visibility that I am aware of. I find myself more conscious of the fact that the collar inspires different expectations in people, and while I would not hesitate to admit my faith if asked on any given day, it is a bit strange to have no one wonder. Which leads me to wonder in what ways I can begin to make my commitment to the Way of Jesus more explicit when I take the collar off. When I do not have anything to mark me as a person of faith, is there anything that might make someone ask me about the hope that is mine?[1] Will people know that I am a disciple of Jesus by my love, or anything else?[2]

The thinker and public theologian Andy Crouch says that if you want to be a radical Christian, then give away 10 percent of your money and watch less TV. It may be that it really doesn't take too much to be weird in the world. I trust that Andy would be quick to note that life with Jesus is about more than our money and our free time—it is just not about less than that. And, in fact, I think he is pointing out just how much we are up against, when it comes to being formed in the Way of Jesus. The idea of giving up 10 percent of our money is enough to make many of us start to twitch, even though tithing has been part of the life of the people of God for millennia. And it's one thing to watch less television, but for those of us who carry entertainment centers in our pockets and live in a world of near constant stimulation, the temptation to distraction is relentless. Mammon and algorithms are insidious stumbling blocks.

Even so, I like the idea that there are seemingly simple things that we can do which prepare us for the great things God is doing. It has always been thus. When the crowds stream out to hear and see John the Baptist in the wilderness, as he prepares the way of the Lord, they are eager to know what they need to do to be ready. John has some pretty basic suggestions: share your stuff generously, don't rip people off or make false accusations, and be satisfied with your wages.[3] Those things hardly seem like the seeds of a holy revolution, but perhaps we overestimate the challenge of living towards the world as God wants it—a world where everyone has enough and no one has too much, a world where honesty and neighborliness are default, a world in which we can be satisfied with enough—and underestimate the influence of small acts of daily faithfulness. Even as we await a new heaven and a new earth, the great gospel reversal and the fullness of God's glory, Jesus consistently describes life in the way of the kingdom with images of smallness: seeds, yeast, coins, fruit, lambs, children. This should probably suggest to us that most of Christian faithfulness consists

---

1. 1 Pet 3:15.
2. John 13:35.
3. Luke 3:10–14.

in simple, daily, often overlooked acts of care, generosity, attention—acts of Christlike love. In the end, the saying holds true: *We can do no great things, only small things with great love.*[4]

What I find consistently unnerving and beautiful in Scripture, is that, from beginning to end, God is determined to have our participation in the stewardship, redemption, renewal, and flourishing of the world, and every voice in the biblical testimony seems to believe we can do it. There is ample evidence that we may not want to, or may choose not to, that this is inefficient and that we will stumble in faithfulness and flag in our commitment to God's will and way. But there is never a question about whether or not we, in all our humanity, are ultimately fit to participate in the new world God is making. When we find ourselves in that glorious new creation, we will be nothing more than our truly human selves. The call of Christ is to grab hold of that humanity now and live it with everything we've got. When Jesus tells us that the most important thing is to love God with all our heart, soul, mind, and strength and to love the things God loves, he offers no qualification that suggests that we are made for anything less, or that any of our faults and failings disqualify us from that pursuit.

Perhaps that is what is so intriguing about Ps 34. We know what a mess David often was. Compared to him, most of our sins seem pretty insignificant. The books of Samuel and Chronicles, where we get David's story, are clear that he was far from perfect. We know that he was no super-human and that there were seasons when it was hard to spot any goodness in him at all. There is a good reason that he knows to pray, "Happy are those whose transgression is forgiven, whose sin is covered."[5] On top of his personal messes, the very context of the Song for the Strange tells us that he knew all about the mess of the world, as much as about its beauty. Somehow, this psalm is connected to a time when he was running for his life, surrounded by enemies, barely surviving. And yet, when push comes to shove, it is praise that flows from his lips. His boast is in the Lord—not his military exploits or the prophetic assurance that he would one day be king, not his wealth or leadership skills, not in his ability to keep his life on track, but in the One who is with him and for him, even in fear and despair, the One who restores him to the joy of salvation, when he wanders far from it.[6]

---

4. This is commonly attributed to Mother Theresa.
5. Ps 32:1.
6. Ps 51:12.

EPILOGUE

David's great gift to us, throughout all of his prayers, is his testimony to the God who is passionately entwined and invested in us and this world—never at a safe and heavenly distance, but always in the thick of life, even when we find ourselves surrounded by enemies and persecutors. It follows that there is nothing in Ps 34 that floats above the ground. It is a vision of life with God, feet firmly planted on the earth, in serenity and storms and everything in between. God will be found not only in pleasant places, but also wherever fear and pain, heartbreak and shame threaten to overwhelm us. This is the same God that had Paul and Silas singing in a jail cell, even as their bodies throbbed from the violence of the world.[7] Even in the depths of a Roman prison, there was never a doubt that they would be heard by the Lord who hears the cries of the righteous. This does not mean that there will not be times and seasons when words fall short, and we find ourselves unable to sing in praise, only that, even then and there, this God will draw near.

And when we discover the nearness of God, our senses are primed for God's goodness, whatever else is going on. To reiterate Norman Wirzba's point, sometimes our willingness to acknowledge the absolute mess and pain of things is precisely the same alertness that we need in order to experience the beauty and abundance of life. The opposite of joy is not sadness, but numbness. David calls us to let our senses be awakened to all that life contains, whether we are crying with broken hearts, or we know exactly what he means by his invitation to taste and see that the Lord is good. Our Jewish siblings can teach us a thing or two about developing the kind of awareness that allows us to taste the goodness of God. Jewish prayers before eating—whether a snack or a meal, for some with every sip of water—are an exercise in holy awareness. The typical prayer goes, "Blessed are you, Lord our God, Ruler of the universe, who creates the fruit of the ground (or vine, tree, nourishment etc.)."[8] Every bite becomes a flare that reminds one of their connection to the Lord and Ruler of the universe. Tingling taste buds point us towards the One who called light out of darkness and cast the stars in the sky, who is God over heights we cannot imagine and Lord of unfathomable smallness. Every morsel can remind us of the One who is with us in joy and pain, and who, in Christ, has offered himself as a feast to satisfy our deepest hungers and thirsts. We can taste the goodness of God.

---

7. Acts 16:16–40.
8. My Jewish Learning, "Blessings for Food and Drink."

Artists and poets like David can help us see the goodness of God more clearly, by doing what they do: showing us the world from an angle or in colors we have never considered before. In the entryway of our apartment hangs a painting by Vancouver artist Julia Soderholm. Julia often paints images from her backyard garden, or everyday scenes in her neighborhood. But she does so in ways that are beautifully disorienting. The painting in our home, called *October*, is evocative of the tangle and overgrowth that often accompanies the end of a growing season. It is full of improbable oranges and blues that compel one to look again and be sure what is there. By choosing to render her garden in colors that most assuredly were not there, she invites us to a deeper attention, an awareness of life that we might overlook. Her series *Neighbourhood Notetaking* accomplishes a similar effect, drawing attention to scenes easily overlooked, but teeming with beauty and life if we will pause to see it.

Poets do with words what visual artists do with physical materials. They reveal a depth and wonder in the world that distraction and disinterest threaten to overwhelm. Poetry turns the stuff of life around, often the most mundane stuff, so that we can see it more clearly and recognize the miraculous intensity of being alive in the world. A poet like William Carlos Williams can make a rain-slicked red wheelbarrow or a couple of plums into vehicles that drive us, startlingly, deep into the beauty and complexity of life.[9] This is part of the reason that the psalms are so important for the church and those of us who would follow Jesus. By choosing to render prayer as poetry and not prose, the pray-ers of the psalter draw us into a dialogue with the whole communion of saints, the generations for whom these words have shaped a vibrant imagination for what it means to live with and for the God who is with and for us. These prayers transcend time and space precisely because they use language in a way that cannot be tied down to one context. When the psalmists say, "The Lord is my shepherd" or that humans are made a little lower than angels, envision mountains singing, or call us to join with everything that has breath in the praise and glory of God, our minds begin to work in a different way than if the psalmists had set out to explain the ways and means of God to us. When they describe themselves as a worm or a child, as sitting in darkness or watching for the morning, filling their bed with tears or joyfully serving in the house of the

---

9. See William Carlos Williams, "This Is Just to Say," and "The Red Wheelbarrow," in Ramazani et al., *Norton*, 294–95. For a good introduction to poetry as an aid in discipleship, see Van Engen, *Word Made Fresh*.

Lord, they open us up to the gamut of human emotion and experience. We have to work at these images, get them into us, let them lead us more than we try to understand them, and when we do, we have a deeper sense of their meaning than straightforward explanation or cool reason will allow.

When David describes God as "a refuge" in Ps 34, we have to allow that to do its work on us. A refuge is both a place of safety and a place of reinvigoration and rest for the next leg of a journey. But, of course, God is not a place, or a structure that we can literally take refuge in. What does it mean to know that God surrounds us, in a way that only God can, working out our safety and security, providing for our needs? How do we enter "into" God? How do we take advantage of God's shelter, or learn to trust God as our shelter, wherever we are and whatever the circumstance? If we learn to know God as a refuge, how can that affect our politics when it comes to refugees? Or our lament, in those times when we feel God's absence more acutely than God's presence? Long paragraphs could be written about what the image of God as a refuge means, but any reader would probably be better served by fifteen minutes of meditation on the image, allowing it to do its work and the Holy Spirit to illuminate what matters in it for this time and place.

One of the wonderful things about Christian discipleship is that we each get to do our own work, trusting the Holy Spirit to speak in us and through us. Neither can we, nor do we have to, let anyone else do this for us. When David summons us to "magnify the Lord with me, and let us exalt his name together," we get to receive that invitation personally. In David's company, and in the Way of Jesus, there is no work that cannot also be praise, there is no circumstance that is not also a sanctuary, there is no life that is insufficient to magnify the Lord—to make God known more and more. The Hebrew word there is *gadal*, which means to cause to grow or make great. In every aspect of our lives, we have a peculiar and improbable capacity to make God bigger in the world, to add to the knowledge of God, to reveal something of the divinity that is the source and sustainer of all life. We are called, daily, into the dynamic, radiant with-God life, part of the throng being gathered to the throne of heaven, ready to thrive in the kingdom of our God.

There are, of course, many aspects of Christian life and faithfulness—perhaps most—that we do not find in Ps 34. It cannot be isolated from the rest of the canon, or the discernment and wisdom of the saints throughout history and in our own communities. It may be designed to be memorized, especially if you happen to read Hebrew, but memorizing it alone will not be enough to keep us moving along the narrow path that leads to life. However, it will give us some resources for the journey. Time spent in Ps 34 is a vigorous introduction to the wonder and glory of God who made us, loves us, and is making us new. Joining David in this boisterous act of praise, full of beauty and promise, will begin to shape us in ways sufficiently strange that we begin to look a bit more like Jesus and the kingdom he proclaimed. It will shape us in ways that make us weird in the world as it is, forming us now for the world as it will be when God gets the world God wants. May it be so.

Bibliography

Aldred, Raymond C., and Matthew R. Anderson. *Our Home on Treaty Land*. Altona, MB: FriesenPress, 2024.
Barker, Mike, dir. *The Handmaid's Tale*. Season 2, episode 2, "Unwomen." Aired April 24, 2018, on Amazon Prime. https://www.primevideo.com/detail/The-Handmaids-Tale/0RC07XHU1VXK97YXW7NNKIGV2U.
Berry, Wendell. *Sex, Economy, Freedom and Community: Eight Essays*. Berkeley: Counterpoint, 2018.
Bonhoeffer, Dietrich. *Discipleship*. Minneapolis: Fortress, 2015.
Bryson, Bill. *A Short History of Nearly Everything: A Journey Through Space and Time*. London: Random House, 2016.
brown, adrienne maree. *Emergent Strategy: Shaping Change, Changing Worlds*. Chico, CA: AK Press, 2017.
Buber, Martin. *I and Thou*. New York: Scribner's, 1958.
Buechner, Frederick. *Beyond Words: Daily Readings in the ABCs of Faith*. New York: HarperOne, 2004.
Chappell, Paul. "The Woke Agenda and Its Influence on Churches and Colleges." Ministry127, March 29, 2023. https://ministry127.com/current-events/the-woke-agenda-and-its-influence-on-churches-and-colleges.
Christian History Institute. "Module 108: Athanasius." https://christianhistoryinstitute.org/uploaded/50ae4a184e3b66.49033776.pdf.
Claiborne, Shane, and Chris Haw. *Jesus for President: Politics for Ordinary Radicals*. Grand Rapids: Zondervan, 2008.
Coakley, Sarah, and SueJeanne Koh. "Prayer as Divine Propulsion: An Interview with Sarah Coakley, Part 1." *The Other Journal*, December 2012. https://theotherjournal.com/2012/12/prayer-as-divine-propulsion-an-interview-with-sarah-coakley/.
Comer, John Mark. *Practicing the Way: Be with Jesus. Become Like Him. Do as He Did*. Colorado Springs: WaterBrook, 2024.
———. "The Prayer Practice." Practicing the Way. https://www.practicingtheway.org/prayer.
———. "The Sabbath Practice." Practicing the Way. https://www.practicingtheway.org/sabbath.
Comer, John Mark, and Andy Crouch. "Luminary Interview: Andy Crouch." *Practicing the Way* podcast, March 19, 2024. https://podcasts.apple.com/ca/podcast/practicing-the-way/id1729195085?i=1000649690020.

BIBLIOGRAPHY

Contemplative Outreach. "Centering Prayer Method." https://www.contemplativeoutreach.org/centering-prayer-method/.

Crawford, Matthew B. *The World Beyond Your Head: On Becoming an Individual in an Age of Distraction*. New York: Farrar, Straus and Giroux, 2016.

Crouch, Andy. *Playing God: Redeeming the Gift of Power*. Downers Grove, IL: InterVarsity, 2013.

Dash, Darryl. "A Quivering Mass of Availability." Dashhouse, November 1, 2006. https://www.dashhouse.com/20061112a-quivering-mass-of-availability-html/.

Del Rosario, Alexandra. "Call Her Suzy: Eddie Izzard Adds to Her Name So Fans 'Can't Make a Mistake.'" *LA Times*, July 23, 2023. http://www.latimes.com/entertainment-arts/story/2023-23-07/eddie-izzard-reveals-new-name-suzy-transgender-comedian.

Foster, Richard J. *Celebration of Discipline: The Path to Spiritual Growth*. New York: HarperOne, 2018.

———. *Prayer: Finding the Heart's True Home*. San Francisco: Harper, 1992.

Guite, Malcolm. *Faith, Hope and Poetry: Theology and the Poetic Imagination*. New York: Routledge, 2016.

Harrison Warren, Tish. *Liturgy of the Ordinary: Sacred Practices in Everyday Life*. Downers Grove, IL: InterVarsity, 2016.

Hauerwas, Stanley. *Jesus Changes Everything: A New World Made Possible*. Walden, NY: Plough, 2025.

Izzard, Eddie. "Christian Singing." YouTube video, November 14, 2010. https://www.youtube.com/watch?v=kuEuY4BUMfM.

Jennings, Willie James. *Acts: A Theological Commentary on the Bible*. Louisville, KY: Westminster John Knox, 2017.

Ladinsky, Daniel. *Love Poems from God: Twelve Sacred Voices from the East and West*. New York: Penguin, 2002.

LeSieur, Simon P. "Come Holy Spirit: Towards a Pneumatologically-Recalibrated Mainline Ecclesiology at West Vancouver United Church." DMin diss., Fuller Theological Seminary, 2022.

Merrill, Nan C. *Psalms for Praying: An Invitation to Wholeness*. London: Bloomsbury, 2007.

Miller, J. Aaron. *Witnesses of These Things: Faithfulness Here and Now*. Eugene, OR: Cascade, 2024.

Morrison, Stephen D. "Happy 130th Birthday, Karl Barth!" May 10, 2016. https://www.sdmorrison.org/happy-130th-birthday-karl-barth/.

The Mortal Atheist. "What Are the Odds of Being Alive?" September 28, 2021. https://www.themortalatheist.com/blog/what-are-the-odds-of-being-alive.

My Jewish Learning. "Blessings for Food and Drink." https://www.myjewishlearning.com/article/blessings-for-food-drink/.

Neander, Joachim. "Praise to the Lord, the Almighty." In *Voices United: The Hymn and Worship Book of the United Church of Canada*, 220. Toronto: The United Church, 1996.

Niclosi, Gary. *Culture Shift: Leading a Growing Church in Uncertain Times*. Bloomington, IN: iUniverse, 2024.

Norris, Kathleen. *The Quotidian Mysteries: Laundry, Liturgy and "Women's Work."* Mahwah, NJ: Paulist, 1998.

Palmer, Parker J. *Let Your Life Speak: Listening for the Voice of Vocation*. Hoboken, NJ: Jossey Bass, 1999.

BIBLIOGRAPHY

Peterson, Eugene H. *Answering God: The Psalms as Tools for Prayer.* New York: HarperOne, 1991.

———. *The Jesus Way: A Conversation on the Ways That Jesus Is the Way.* Grand Rapids: Eerdmans, 2007.

———. *A Long Obedience in the Same Direction: Discipleship in an Instant Society.* Downers Grove, IL: InterVarsity, 2000.

———. *The Message: The Bible in Contemporary Language, Numbered Edition.* Colorado Springs: NavPress, 2005.

———. *Practice Resurrection: A Conversation on Growing Up in Christ.* Grand Rapids: Eerdmans, 2013.

Prado, Adélia. "Serenade." In *Zero at the Bone: Fifty Entries Against Despair*, by Christian Wiman, 60. New York: Farrar, Straus and Giroux, 2023.

Prior, Karen Swallow. *The Evangelical Imagination: How Stories, Images, and Metaphors Created a Culture in Crisis.* Grand Rapids: Brazos, 2023.

Psihoyos, Louie, dir. *Mission: Joy—Finding Happiness in Troubled Times.* Los Gatos, CA: Netflix, 2021.

Ramazani, Jahan, et al., eds. *The Norton Anthology of Modern and Contemporary Poetry.* Vol. 1: *Modern Poetry*. New York: Norton, 2003.

Raphael, Frederic. *A Jew Among Romans: The Life and Legacy of Flavius Josephus.* New York: Pantheon, 2013.

Riley, Cole Arthur. *Black Liturgies: Prayers, Poems, and Meditations for Staying Human.* New York: Convergent, 2024.

Rowe, C. Cavin. *Leading Christian Communities.* Grand Rapids: Eerdmans, 2023.

Sanctuary Mental Health Course. "Session 5: Companionship." https://portal.sanctuarymental health.org/the-sanctuary-course/session-5.

Skogland, Kari, dir. *The Handmaid's Tale.* Season 2, episode 4, "Other Women." Aired May 8, 2018, on Amazon Prime. https://www.primevideo.com/detail/The-Handmaids-Tale/0RC07XHU1VXK97YXW7NNKIGV2U.

Smith, Gordon T. *Called to Be Saints: An Invitation to Christian Maturity.* Downers Grove, IL: InterVarsity Academic, 2013.

Smith, James K. A. *Awaiting the King: Reforming Public Theology.* Cultural Liturgies 3. Grand Rapids: Baker Academic, 2017.

———. *How (Not) to Be Secular: Reading Charles Taylor.* Grand Rapids: Eerdmans, 2014.

Staton, Tyler. "Reviving the Ancient Practice of a Rule of Life." The Way Church, March 13, 2023. https://vimeo.com/807659756.

Taylor, Charles. *A Secular Age.* Cambridge, MA: Belknap, 2007.

Thompson, Curt. *The Deepest Place: Suffering and the Formation of Hope.* Grand Rapids: Zondervan, 2023.

Tyson, Jon, and Heather Grizzle. *A Creative Minority: Influencing Culture Through Redemptive Participation.* New York, 2016.

Van Engen, Abram. *Word Made Fresh: An Invitation to Poetry for the Church.* Grand Rapids: Eerdmans, 2024.

Villodas, Rich. *The Deeply Formed Life: Five Transformative Values to Root Us in the Way of Jesus.* Colorado Springs: WaterBrook, 2020.

Wesley, John. *Voices United: The Hymn and Worship Book of the United Church of Canada.* Toronto: The United Church, 1996.

Willimon, William H. *Remember Who You Are: Baptism, a Model for Christian Life.* Nashville: Upper Room, 1980.

BIBLIOGRAPHY

Wilson-Hartgrove, Jonathan. *New Monasticism: What It Has to Say to Today's Church.* Grand Rapids: Brazos, 2008.

Wirzba, Norman. *Love's Braided Dance: Hope in a Time of Crisis.* New Haven, CT: Yale University Press, 2024.

www.ingramcontent.com/pod-product-compliance
Lightning Source LLC
Chambersburg PA
CBHW020855160426
43192CB00007B/942